Horus Templar

and the

Case of the Dubious Decedent

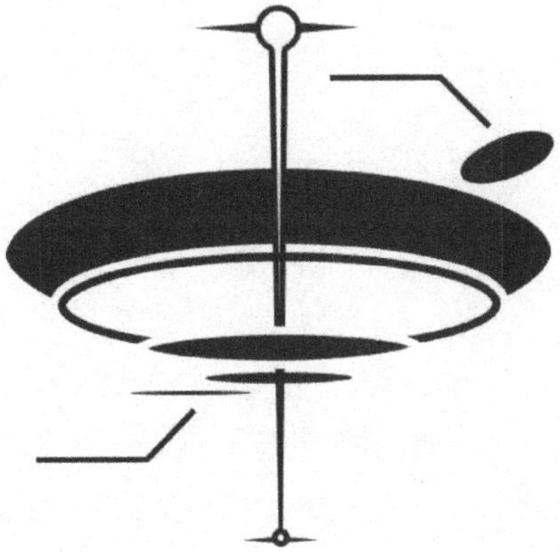

E.L. WARD

ISBN: 978-1-7370436-3-8

Table of Contents

"You imagine the world is discordant, and that is what makes it so."

- Magormissahr, *Referendums on the World, Vol. 1042*

Chapter 1

Never in the history of the world had there been a more ordinary day in court. The prosecuting attorney Orville Buttersworth summoned one perfectly commonplace St. Argonsburgite after another to relate their mundane experiences before judge and jury, while Horus Templar sprinkled in objections to taste. Appeals were sustained and overruled with relative equity. Neither testimony nor points of procedure ever strayed deeper than the foamy shores of controversy. It was a clean, fairly-officiated, unprepossessing sort of battle, devoid of scandal or sudden outrage...

In retrospect, that should've been the first warning sign.

"And when you heard these remarks of Ms. Elena, what was your immediate reaction?" Mr. Buttersworth asked.

"I turned and left," the witness shrugged. "There didn't seem any sense doing business with Mr. Knotts if he botched a job half as bad as she said he did. Figured I'd try my luck someplace else."

The seasoned old litigator nodded his low-hanging face as he gripped his brown, striped suit-jacket, somehow looking more like a train conductor than a lawyer. "Thank you, Sir. I have no further questions."

Horus stood, even as Buttersworth returned to his seat. "No questions on cross," he announced.

Judge Felix's face bunched up in a tired look, just as Horus had seen it do with increasing frequency each time their legal careers happened to overlap. "Mr. Templar," he began with a sigh, "I can't help noting that you have not examined *any* of Mr. Buttersworth's witnesses thus far. Do you intend to present a defense, at least? Or should your client avail herself of her privilege to seek other counsel?"

Horus angled a quick look down at Elena, who did appear rather doubtful herself. He hoped his answer would reassure them both...

"With respect, your Honor, I believe the successful defense of this case rests not in disproving the damaging nature of my client's statements, but rather, on demonstrating their verity. Slander – as your Honor knows well – must be both harmful and untrue. It is our contention that Mr. Knotts' agency conducts its business in a manner worthy of my client's criticism. And it is in that spirit that I intend to present a defense."

"I see," Judge Felix replied. He turned to Elena. "Does the defendant find this satisfactory?"

She nodded, and Horus was glad to see she looked more confident. "Yes, your Honor."

"Very good." The judge looked back to Buttersworth. "The prosecution may call his next witness."

Buttersworth stood in address. "The prosecution rests, your Honor."

"Then let the defense present its case, as promised." He clacked his gavel lightly for good measure, as if still feeling some responsibility to restrain Horus from unexpected mischief. Horus only grinned and turned to face the plaintiff.

"I call Mr. Berry Knotts to the stand."

The suing business owner stood, managing not to appear especially anxious or relaxed. The court officer intercepted him in the modest emptiness between his table and the stand, just like always...

"State your name," he recited mechanically.

A grin neither cleverly devious nor vacantly simple curled up one side of Mr. Knotts' plain, ageless face. He volunteered a reply as autonomic as the officer's command. "Beryllium Knotts."

...And just then – when all seemed securely tucked into the deepest fastness of the status quo – an errant sound shouldered headlong into the cogs of orderly existence...

"*Boooo*!"

The collective hearts of everyone in the courtroom skipped a beat.

Boo?

Horus reeled. Had someone really just *booed*? He couldn't account for crowd noise like that in such a serious setting. The penalty for civil slander was only a question of money... that was all that was at stake now between the litigants. But for contempt of court – even small claims – the sentence was death. Who could be so canted, so oblivious, or so possessed of a death wish as to *boo*, here and now? Horus was aware of himself looking around the room, in much the same way he might check for space aliens. He knew he couldn't have merely imagined the jeer. After all, everyone else was searching just as he was...

After his own failed attempt to pinpoint the source of the *boo*, Judge Felix struck the bench. "There will be no more outbursts in this court," he commanded, sounding more amazed than officious. "We will have order."

At length, the court officer cleared his throat, finally remembering himself. He turned his eyes back on Knotts and continued. "Do you swear to tell the truth, so help ye Creators?"

"I do," Knotts replied weakly, standing tense as if he might need to duck out of the way of another ballistic faux pas. But the court was silent.

"Be seated," the officer finished, feeling a quick rush of relief that he was not interrupted a second time. He was not the only one. The whole chamber resumed breathing, seeing the aberrant moment had passed...

For his part, Horus didn't miss his cue by so much as a beat, arriving before the stand just as Knotts seated himself behind it. "Let us begin with the obvious, Mr. Knotts," he said. "You are the operator, owner, and originator of Slipshod Logistics Consultancy, is that not so?"

Knotts nodded rather confidently. "I am, and proud to say so. My company has a proven history of serving customers." For reasons of his own, he chose this moment as ideal for a shameless plug. "Slipshod Logistics – where anything worth doing once is worth doing all over again."

"*Bah*!" the anonymous naysayer called again, his voice ricocheting off the walls. "*Phooey*! *Gak*!"

As before, the whole assembly was set abuzz with hushed alarm, ironically camouflaging the bad egg in the chaos of swiveling faces. Felix unleashed a series of angry little hammer-strokes...

"Enough!" the judge insisted. "Enough of this! We are in a court of law, not a travelling side-show! If I hear so much as one more peep out of turn, the offender *will* be found, and forcibly evicted." He was being gracious. His gaze turned up to the back of the chamber. "The bailiff will come forward, where he can keep an eye on the crowd."

The bailiff obliged, his stern and impassive front compromised somewhat. It was clear he'd never been asked to do this sort of thing before.

Felix turned back to Horus with an even more tired look. "Please proceed, Mr. Templar."

Horus nodded. "Very well, your Honor." He set an elbow on the stand, quickly and expertly jousting the plaintiff with his eyes, just as if nothing had happened. "Let me see if I caught that catch-phrase of yours correctly: 'Anything worth doing once is worth doing all over again'?"

"That's right," Knotts confirmed.

"I find it most interesting that you would volunteer your company slogan here and now, Mr. Knotts. For a business built on helping other businesses organize their workflow, I wouldn't say it inspires much confidence."

Knotts shrugged. "Slogans are supposed to be catchy."

"They also generally convey something of a company's virtue. Tell me, Mr. Knotts: Does Slipshod Logistics presume to provide *quality* service to its customers?"

"No," Knotts answered unequivocally. "We offer help to people trying to organize themselves. I never said it was good help."

"Then your slogan isn't so much a slogan at all, as it is a disclaimer?"

"You could say that."

At this juncture, Horus grinned mischievously. "With respect, then, Mr. Knotts: Why prefer charges against my client? You admit your work is sloppy, do you not?"

"I do."

"Then the remarks made by my Ms. Elena are not so much defamatory as they are simply accurate. Why not rather think of what she said as free advertising?"

Knotts shook his head. "Advertising I don't need, Mr. Templar. You'll appreciate the difference. The slogan works well enough so long as people don't think very hard about what it means."

"Ah. I begin to see your angle, I believe," Horus replied. He looked up at Judge Felix. "Your Honor, I motion for a dismissal. The plaintiff himself has just admitted that the damaging remarks of my client reliably characterize his business."

Felix turned to Buttersworth. "How would the prosecution answer?"

Buttersworth stood. "Respectfully, your Honor, I would say Mr. Templar's motion is somewhat premature. It is, of course, the express opinion of the defendant that Slipshod Logistics conducts poor business. And the plaintiff admits that he does not – as a matter of subjective policy – tend to exert himself to a very high standard. But that does not in itself *prove* a history of bad service. There is no corroborating testimony. Let Mr. Templar produce an objective source who will confirm that Slipshod Logistics deserves its black mark, before we give any thought to dismissal."

Felix shifted back to Horus. "Is the defense prepared to produce a corroborating witness?"

"I am, your Honor."

The judge nodded. "Then I do believe it would be in order for you to do so."

"*Boo*! ***Boooo***!" the ineffable heckler in the court called out. Only this time, there was no missing him. He stood and cupped his hands as he blustered on. "Send him up the river! Make 'im eat dirt!"

"Order!" Felix commanded through his gavel-thumping. "You there! You've been warned repeatedly to refrain from these outbursts! Bailiff, seize that man and throw him out at once!"

Horus tugged at his shirt collar, eyes wide and teeth clenched. As much as anyone, he would've liked to see this peculiar disruption neatly dispelled. But he was rather surprised – and more than a little stymied – seeing who it was causing all the mischief. Watching the bailiff close the distance, he could only faintly flinch while he deliberated what to do about it, if anything. Finally, he knew he could find no way around speaking up...

"Your Honor," he ventured. "I know this is highly irregular... but I must beg the court's forbearance."

Judge Felix regarded Horus with wide eyes. "Forbearance? What do you mean, Counselor?"

Horus strained not to avert his eyes to his knitted fingers. "I must insist that this man not be removed from court."

The judge motioned for the bailiff to hold, perhaps despite himself. But of course, he had to know...

"Why, Mr. Templar? Why should this man not be ejected at once?"

Horus examined the man, who looked just as confounded as anyone. Then he turned back to Felix, face wiggly with an apologetic grin...

"Regrettably, your Honor, he is my next witness."

* * *

"Now Mr. Tweed..." Horus began, finding renewed confidence as he discovered his unruly little witness had been thoroughly cowed. Far from the fist-waving hooligan of a few moments prior, Tweed sat hunched and bug-eyed behind the stand, slick with that distinctly Human whole-body sweat. In fact, if he was dangerously bold before, he may've gone too far in the other direction. More than put in his place, Tweed looked terrified...

"...approximately three months prior," Horus continued, "you were sent by the foreign Embassy to recruit Mr. Knotts' assistance in organizing a public gala, is that correct?"

Tweed gulped audibly. "...I... I..."

"Objection!" cried Berry Knotts. The accusatory eyes of both judge and prosecutor snapped onto him...

Felix set his gavel to work again. "Now *you* are out of order, Mr. Knotts," he intoned. "It is for your legal representative to object."

"Sorry, Judge," Knotts dared continue. "But Mr. Templar doesn't have any right to bring up the Embassy job! That was before I reincorporated my company as Slipshod Logistics Consultancy. It was handled by the now-defunct Slapdash Coordination Services."

"You may've changed the name over the door," Horus retorted, "but that falls rather short of legal reincorporation."

"...Oh," Knotts whimpered.

Horus produced some ominous-looking papers. "It's all here, Mr. Knotts. Shall I have the court assess your handling of your own corporate entity, or may I continue?"

Buttersworth stood up, staring his own client down. "The *plaintiff* withdraws his remarks," he announced.

"Very good," Judge Felix remarked, massaging his head. He sighed in Horus' general direction. "Please go on, Mr. Templar."

"Yes, your Honor." He turned to Tweed. "Now, Mr. Tweed... about that gala. Did you not approach Mr. Knotts on the Embassy's behalf?"

Tweed didn't so much as blink. His eyes appeared increasingly unable to fit into their sockets. "I..." he said. "...I..."

Horus tried to be patient with Tweed... to give him time to work past this strange funk he seemed to be in. But after a prolonged silence, he decided his witness might not even be able to continue without some coaching...

"Mr. Tweed," he began lightly, "there's nothing for you to fear. The judge has excused your contempt of court, so that you may testify."

"...I..." he replied. "...I don't want to."

The crowd murmured. Horus himself was incredulous. The cowed Tweed was quickly becoming as troublesome as the raucous one. There wasn't so much as a click from Felix's gavel – he appeared resigned to whatever weirdness was to come. It was up to Horus alone to keep this thing moving somehow...

"You *have* to, Mr. Tweed," Horus urged him, gentle but firm. "I have only a few simple questions."

Suddenly, something snapped inside of Tweed. He fixed an angrier, uglier look on Horus. "A few? Simple? Questions? Don't sound so innocent, Mr. Templar. Don't you think I know what you're doing, calling me up here? You're trying to trip me up! You're backing me into a corner! I don't know how exactly, but I can see you setting the trap. You're a tricky one, alright. But you won't get *me*! I *refuse*!!" he exclaimed. "I refuse to answer! I refuse to incriminate myself!"

Horus half-winced, half-gaped. "You... don't seem to understand what we're engaged in at all. We're assessing the work of Mr. Knotts. How do you propose to incriminate *yourself*?" He was to immediately regret asking such an ungermane question...

Tweed folded his arms. "There you go... right for the jugular! You'd like me to spill it all, wouldn't you? The whole mess. Every gruesome detail." He laughed mirthlessly. "But then, listen to me... I've all-but confessed already." He stood up, a picture of fatalistic defiance. "Very well, Mr. Templar, you win. You caught me after all. *I did it*."

Horus was beside himself. He looked to Judge Felix, who was no help... even if he'd obviously reengaged with the drama. His features were arrested with dread-curiosity while he waited for something coherent to come out of Tweed's mouth. Something Horus was obliged to mine for, now... no matter how irrelevant and immaterial it might be to this simple slander case...

"What are you talking about?" He trained *that look* on Tweed... the *look* that only a courtroom genius could ever truly master... the one that could draw the truth out of a bastion of lies and secrets...

Tweed's eyes flared with a crazed fire. "Didn't you *hear* me? I DID IT!!!" He wildly pounded his vague revelation into the railing of the stand. "I DID IT, I DID IT, I DID IT!!!"

At this point, Horus needed the answer as much as anyone. He dialed his *look* up to maximum firepower. "Did what?"

"You ***know*** what!!" he said, before looking up into the crowd. "I killed him!" Tweed revealed at last, his whole body convulsing with the force of the words. "I killed him!"

Chapter 2

The dark little interrogation room had the air of a war-council as Horus stepped inside. Meager lamplight carved the contours of grim expressions aimed his way. Hamilton Blackforest and Blucille Cordon stood up – their body language as standoffish as their faces. Being a perceptive fellow, Horus got the distinct impression they weren't happy to see him. Blackforest's greeting confirmed as much...

"A fine mess you've got us into this time, Horus," he said.

Horus blanched, exchanging a wounded look with Deborah. He held a hand up against himself. "*Me*? Why are we making this *my* fault? I didn't kill anyone!"

"But you would just *have* to find the one material witness in the whole country who did," Blucille huffed.

"Not on purpose! Believe me, I was as surprised as anyone!"

"That was hardly the impression Judge Felix left," Blackforest weighed back in. "To hear him talk, it was 1st degree dramaturgy with intent to derail. Anyway you've pulled wild stunts in his court before... he made that abundantly clear."

"That certainly *sounds* like someone we know," Deputy Constable Stenya Miloje commented – calmly seated beside his honor guard and understudy, Captain Alexei – while a devious grin curled his mustache.

"Enough'a that!" Art Mallard said between puffs on his pipe. Horus had little noted his friend's presence, half-sitting on the end of the table with his back to the door. "Are we just here to throw Horus under the bus, or are we gonna talk business? If he says he didn't know, he didn't know."

"Well he must've suspected *something*," Blackforest rejoined, leveling another glare at Horus. "He ought to own up to it, instead of coming in here, pleading his ignorance."

Horus was at a loss for more cues of pure bewilderment. "What do you want from me, Hamilton? What more can I say? I swear, I hadn't the foggiest idea I was putting a killer on the stand!"

"Then what kind of witness *did* you suppose you were calling on?" Blucille asked, putting a hand on her hip. "You met with this Tweed at the Embassy. Naturally you interviewed him prior to making him part of your case. You're a man of some discernment, Templar. Your man Tweed – on the other hand – is a certifiable maniac! Would you have us believe you didn't notice?"

The question had Horus looking back to Deborah for support. Oddly, the way she mirrored his blindsided expression helped somewhat. "They did warn me he was a bit... *eccentric*," Horus replied slowly, as he turned back to the board of inquiry. "And yes, there were a few off-color moments in the interview. Canted metaphors, unusual tics. But mostly, I saw what I went there looking for: a man displeased with the service of Slapdash Coordination. If he was lucid enough at the time to convey that much, then I hope I can be forgiven for it."

By this time, Deborah had already gone fishing in her briefcase. "I have the transcript from the interview right here." She proffered it at Ms. Cordon. "Since you ardently *refuse* to take Horus at his word, I suggest you look it over." Horus was grateful... if a bit surprised at her. Deborah's fair, dauntless voice was edged with a combative undertow.

Blucille seemed to notice as well. She accepted the transcript with some crestfallen hesitance. But her eyes rushed to meet the paper, and at once she was worlds away.

"In any event, I fear Mr. Mallard is right," Captain Alexei segued. "This muckraking is getting us nowhere. A matter of this import demands real cooperation."

Import? Horus mused. He took a fresh look around the room. There was the District Attorney and his pupil... and the Deputy Constable and *his* pupil... not only the top brass of St. Argonsburg's law enforcement, but their respective runners-up as well. And if that wasn't enough, Art was also present – the city's premier private investigator. Each of them was a friend and associate whom he was more than accustomed to seeing. But to have them all assembled for this one case? Killings were certainly rare, and heinous. But this was far too much heat to bring for any mere civil matter...

"Today must be the day for outing myself as an ignoramus," he said. "Why *are* we all here? I confess I don't see the need. Any ADA can handle a murder case."

For a long moment, Blackforest could only glower. "It's *Tweed*, Horus... if that wasn't perfectly obvious before." His eyes narrowed with new suspicion. "What exactly *did* you know, the day you went to the Embassy?"

Horus slouched, growing very weary of being hit in the backside with this particular revolving door. But he rallied, drew a breath, and answered calmly. "I knew a man named Beryllium Knotts – a man suing a client of mine for slander – had once been consulted to help organize a public gala at the Embassy... a gala that turned out to be a grand embarrassment. That is *all* I knew going in. I went up to their front desk and merely asked the name of the party that had been in contact with Mr. Knotts. They gave me the name Archie Tweed. The rest has already been submitted to you." He turned his hands up, as if there was any more he could do to clear himself. "I assumed he was a simple functionary at the Embassy. I take it I was... *mistaken*."

Blackforest nodded. "That you were. Oh, the people that run the Embassy give him odd jobs... probably to keep him out of their hair. But he's no functionary, Horus. He's a *resident*."

Horus sighed, running a hand over his head. "*Of course*. That would make this something of an international incident." He searched the DA. "But surely he's not an *ambassador*... not if he's as crazy as you say."

Blackforest turned a rather sickly look past the still-speedreading Ms. Cordon over to Miloje, who only shrugged with pursed lips. Begrudgingly, he returned to Horus. "Well, now I feel as if you've called *my* bluff. You're right... he's no ambassador. But truth be told, we don't have a fix on exactly who he *is* yet. All we could get out of the embassy is that he's a former close relation of one of their most distinguished boarders."

Horus' brows knit. "*Former*? How can you be *formerly* related to anyone?"

"Maybe it's like one of those 'third-cousin-twice-removed' deals," Art supposed. Horus fairly ignored him, pressing Hamilton for answers with his eyes...

"Well blast it, Horus, *I don't know*!" Blackforest forced through his fangs. "And I'm not about to press the issue. If our foreign envoys are inclined to distance themselves from Tweed, I can't say I blame them. Anyway, barking up the family tree isn't about to solve the real problem here... it only runs the risk of offending important diplomats."

Horus twiddled his claws through his chin-hair thoughtfully. "But don't we need to check into his background? At the very least, to determine whether he has an immunity status?"

Blackforest shook his head. "The Czarina wants Tweed tried... and sentenced, to the full extent of the law. Her office intends to waive any such status. Even *she* feels that the peasantry ought to have some assurances in life. Namely, that they can't be killed-off without at least some demonstrable provocation. Not even by moderately important people."

"So then, what's the problem? Apparently, you already have the Czarina's blessing. Simply put Tweed on trial."

"We can't," Blucille interjected, still reading away. But she looked up then, driving her point home. "We have no case."

Art Mallard blew a decompressing breath as he sat down his pipe. "Which is to say, they have no *victim*."

Horus was aghast. He fixed his shock on Blackforest. "Is this true? You haven't learned *who* he killed?"

Blackforest sank back down into his seat. "It's true," he answered in a low voice. "But not for lack of trying. We've been through the whole good-cop-bad-cop routine. We're about to turn Art and half the SAPD loose on every remotely suspicious death we can dig up. But the trail is cold. There hasn't been a missing person report in weeks – nothing that clearly resembles a killing in *months*. And we can't get Tweed to talk." He paused then, in just such a way that made the words to follow rather redundant. "That's where you come in."

Horus laughed nervously despite himself. "Oh, I don't think so, Hamilton. You're not making me Tweed's attorney."

"Aren't I?" Blackforest challenged.

"It's a clear conflict of interest," Horus explained. "He's a witness in a case I'm already working. I can't represent someone who materially affects the trial of another client."

Blackforest smiled. People often wondered how he could smile like that without cutting his own jowls off. "I think you'll find that case is closed, Horus. Knotts dropped all charges an hour ago. He didn't want to be connected with this killing scandal either. And I think he knew you had him dead to rights, the moment you were able to tie one of his old corporations into the case."

Horus shook his head, sighing. "Well, I suppose that settles that. So much for the spoils of victory. But I hope you won't let Knotts slip away too quietly. His eagerness to distance himself from the killing could indicate a connection worth covering up."

"We'll see where the evidence leads us," Miloje retorted with a dismissive shrug. "I rather doubt he's an accessory. But for now, rest assured we have him under surveillance." He leaned over the table, with a fresh, mocking glint in his eye. "Your concern now should be for your new *client*."

"*Right*," Horus breathed, hopeless to feign anything besides aggravation. This was the worst part of the job... having to represent guilty clients. Rumor had it that somewhere out there, perhaps beyond the confines of infinity, a select few defense attorneys – the likes of which shall here remain nameless – enjoyed the unforgivable good luck of going through their entire careers without ever representing a single miscreant. Horus could only envy them. True, some of his most endearing clients had actually committed crimes – men and women with genuine remorse – and for these few, he had fought more fervently than for most. But this was no Inquisitor who had pocketed a bit of gold in a moment of weakness, or unassuming Clerk with the misfortune of getting caught in an international conspiracy. This was a *killer*... and evidently, a deranged one. He didn't have high hopes of developing a deep rapport...

"I'll go and see him presently," Horus continued. "But first, I'd like to be sure I'm up-to-speed. Did you learn anything from your interrogation that I should know about?"

Even with a room half-full of experienced law-enforcement raconteurs, Horus' question seemed to fall right into a sonic void.

"...Apparently not," Horus surmised at length.

"It was mostly a lot of nonsense," Blucille finally admitted. "That is, when we could get him to speak at all." She reached for some papers of her own. "Perhaps you'd like to review *our* transcripts," she offered.

Deborah reached. "I'll take those, thank you."

Horus noted Captain Alexei thoughtfully rub his chin, just before he spoke up. "There was that bit of forensic evidence. Nothing conclusive, of course... only highly circumstantial. Even so, perhaps the Doctor ought to fill you in."

"The Doctor?" Horus asked, getting a sinking feeling. The SAPD had a whole medical staff, each member of which had names – names that were easy to remember. There was only one person that anyone would bother to refer to with ominous vagueness as "The Doctor". And, much as he had an unpleasant time or two before, Horus suddenly *sensed* another presence in the room. "You mean...?"

"Yes. I am here, too," Dr. Nokkaeru replied, stepping out of deep shadows she had no good reason to skulk in in the first place. "And why should you wonder? A mystery such as this demands the very best minds your quaint police department has to offer."

"Apparently," Horus was obliged to nod. "But now, I'm almost afraid to ask... how did *you* get any information on Tweed?" He couldn't help his face scrunching a bit. "I do hope you didn't... carve it out of him."

The Heron physician turned up an empty talon. "Had I been permitted such latitudes, we would not be here now, but alas. I can only report what I was able to observe on the surface. Chiefly, I noted significant bruising along the forearms and the hypothenar eminence of the right hand."

At mention of this anatomical reference, Horus was vaguely aware that Art shuddered. But he went on mulling it over. "Bruising, you say. So, the evidence points to a recent killing?"

Nokkaeru nodded. "Quite likely within the last two weeks – but I would expect it was very recent – no more than a few days ago."

Horus arrived at another uncomfortable conclusion. "Do you suppose he beat the other man to death with his bare hands?"

"I make it very doubtful," she assessed. "His knuckles were not badly damaged, where in such a case they should've been bruised and scabbed over."

"So then, he used a weapon?"

She shook her head. "That I deem even more unlikely. I could find no trace of foreign blood. Stabbings are a messy business. Even after very thorough washing and scrubbing, I suspect I would have found *something*. Skin and hair hold onto more debris than they are often given credit for."

"But what about a gun?"

"The least plausible of all. I can test for gunshot residue. The powder explosion leaves chemicals in the skin. This Tweed person would've had no hope at all of cleaning it away in such a short time."

"So, what does that leave?" Horus pressed, coming up empty on causes of death.

"My strongest suspicion is strangulation," she revealed. "It is consistent with all the evidence – the undamaged posterior of the hands, the lack of blood or powder residue. The victim would have likely beat on Mr. Tweed's arms in an attempt to free himself, which accounts for the bruising along them."

Horus stared stoically into space as he considered it. It painted a grim picture indeed – seemingly irrefutable for all its forensic cues. Though there remained one trifle… one impossibly unremarkable question he nevertheless decided to venture. "And what about the bruise on the hand?"

Here, the Doctor might've shrugged if she'd had shoulders. "If the victim's clavicle was pressed against it with sufficient force, his hand could conceivably have been bruised in such a way. But you must remember: All of this is educated inference. The burden of truth rests squarely with you.

However, if you would like my help in extracting it, perhaps together we may yet persuade the authorities to make an allowance for the use of extraordinary measures."

Horus managed an insincere grin as he shook his head. "I don't think so, Doctor. If you want another crack at Tweed, I suggest taking it up with someone who *isn't* his defense attorney."

"Suit yourself, Counselor," she replied, turning her beak up. "But if you're going to be that way about it, then I suppose my part here is played. I have other duties." She turned her mirrored goggles on Blackforest. "May I be excused?"

"Certainly," he was quick to confirm.

To what seemed collective relief, she started for the door. "Very well. I take my leave. A pleasure, as always, to see you, Mr. Templar. You and your dear secretary." She stopped just before Horus, shooting a last look up at him – fawning as it was ominous, though he couldn't see her eyes. "Your dear, *dear* secretary." And just like that, she started on her way again...

Horus fought an impulse to tug at his collar, and another impulse to swallow his tongue. Not so long ago, Dr. Nokkaeru had come into possession of certain compromising data – namely, the secret of Horus' feelings for Deborah. And now, if the broadcast a moment ago was any clue, she appeared to have every intention of making him pay dearly for it. She was going to take what she knew and dangle it in open forum. Horus could only silently dread her newfound power to casually ruin his life, though the urge to nervously snicker was overwhelming...

Fortunately, Alexei cleared his throat, corralling Horus' attention before he could get too lost in the contemplation of his doom. All eyes turned to the police captain. "As a matter of fact, I'm going to have to hoof it now, too," he said, a foreboding expression trained on his pocket watch. Without so much as asking permission, his long legs began to carry him away. "Begging your pardon, my fellows and superiors. I've urgent business across town that can't wait."

"That's news to *me*," replied the Deputy Constable.

Alexei didn't break stride... if anything, he was still picking up speed. "I'm terribly sorry. You'll find my excusal on your desk." He flung the door open and was gone.

"*Excusal*," Miloje huffed. "What the devil has gotten into him? Does he suppose he can come and go as he chooses now, just because he is a shoo-in for my job?"

"Strange," Blackforest mused. "Alexei's never shown any insubordination before. Whatever it is that's carried him off, I'm sure it's important."

"It had better be. The last I checked, walking off the job is still a capital offense."

"Well, if I read the horrified look on his face the right way, he should be able to account for his absence alright," Blucille stated surely. "Anyway, we *all* have other business. Can we just get this meeting over with?"

"Here, here," Miloje agreed. "The search for the slain man is about to commence. I should be there... particularly if our good Captain is otherwise engaged."

Blackforest looked at him quizzically. "You have plenty of other policemen, Stenya. There's no need to go kicking down doors personally."

The witty twinkle in Miloje's eyes rekindled. "Your own orders were to send every able-bodied man I could spare. Which, if you've forgotten, once again includes me," he intoned. It had been some months already since his miraculous recovery from heart arrythmia, and yet he still managed to be smug as a kingpin about it.

"As if you'd *let* us forget," Blackforest quipped. "Go ahead, then. Blucille and I can handle what little business remains here."

Miloje stood – tipped his bobby. "Adieu, then, my comrades. And goodwill hunting." Then he too left, in a sauntering sort of way.

"I almost miss the feeble invalid," the DA grumbled when Miloje had gone, shaking his head. "Where were we?"

"I wondered that myself," Horus admitted. "You've given me my assignment... brought me up to speed. What does that leave?"

"It leaves the *deadline*," Blucille boded.

"Deadline, you say?" Horus inquired. "What sort of deadline?"

"Well, thanks to certain new statutes of limitations – proposed by parties I'm sure I have no need to name here..." Blackforest growled, "...we can't hold Tweed indefinitely without trying him. Until we have a corpse, we can only hold him on suspicion. And we can only do that for three more days."

Art whistled. "*Three days*," he repeated. "Hot dog. You'll be turning a lunatic loose just in time for the Syzygy."

SNAP!

A loud fracturing sound emanated just then from the clipboard where Deborah had been taking notes. Their collective ears and eyes fixed on her...

"Sorry," she said. "I broke the lead on my pencil."

"...You're using a pen," Horus pointed out meekly.

"Oh, so I am!" she laughed it off. "Not to worry – I have another one right here."

Horus found himself considering her with a bit of bewilderment. But in the next second, Blackforest rejoined the discussion...

"Well, I'd like to say I'm disappointed, Art. But honestly, it would be just like you to point out something so perfectly irrelevant as the *Syzygy*."

"But it's *not* irrelevant," Blucille argued. "Not to the extent it alarms the layman. If anything, Art just did us a favor. He proved what we've been fearing – what the Czarina fears: that the people will imagine some connection between the Syzygy and our turning out a known killer."

"Since when do we care what the people *imagine*?" Blackforest demanded. "The Syzygy's just a lot of hogwash! It's just an eventuality of everyday astronomy that people attach a lot of baseless superstition to!"

"Don't count on it, Mac," Art cautioned. "We're talking about four different worlds here... all lining up in a row! Surely that would have to have *some* kinda messed-up effect on the fabric of space-time. Otherwise, what's the point?"

"*Oh for Heck's sake*," Blackforest sighed, burying his face in hands and long claws.

"Well, never mind," Blucille insisted. "Astrological manifestations or no, the fact remains we have *three days*." She focused on Horus. "Get in there and resolve this thing, Templar. Make Tweed see reason, if that's even possible. I don't think any of us wants to find out what the Czarina will do if we can't make the charges stick."

Horus tugged out the cuffs of his shirt. "Thank you for that grim ultimatum. I'll see what I can do."

Chapter 3

"I just need to blabber on and on," Horus said. Or anyway, he might as well have said that, for all Deborah managed to absorb, just then...

"M-hm," he heard her agree.

"Of course, I'd expect nothing else from Hamilton," he continued. "He's as brilliant as they come, but he has that tendency to not pursue the facts any farther than it suits him, wherever there could be controversy. I can understand wanting to avoid trouble, but not at the price of negligence."

"Right."

"The fact of the matter is, we'll almost certainly have to go poking around the Embassy. If this meeting goes badly – and I expect it will – finding out Tweed's origins may be the only means we have of arriving at a plausible motive, to say nothing of the actual victim."

"Yup."

Horus looked down at her. "Are you getting all this, Deborah? I haven't heard the pen on paper in some time..."

Her eyes bugged – she averted her gaze. "Sorry, Boss. I guess I spaced out a bit, there."

He shrugged it off. "Well, no matter. With the slander case laid to rest, our schedule's an open book. We can head straight to the Embassy from here, if need be." He grinned at her wryly. "Then again, we might just want to get lunch first. I've heard tell of a butchery near the consulate district that's struggling to make ends meet, and they've started selling more interesting cuts... parts of the animal Humans thoughtlessly discard everywhere else! Moose nose... diplodocus brains..."

Faintly, Horus detected a sound almost like a groan. "Maybe some other time," Deborah replied weakly.

At once, his vague misgivings blossomed into genuine concern. "Deborah, are you sure you're feeling alright? You haven't seemed quite yourself today."

"Is it that obvious?" she sighed. "I *am* feeling a little under the weather. I'm sorry, Horus; I should've told you."

"A head-cold?"

"Something like that, I'd like to think."

He nodded, smiling confidently. "Well, don't worry. In a few short, eventful days, I'm sure everything will be back to normal."

"I certainly hope you're right about that," she said – rather more ominously than she might've, Horus felt...

But just then, they pushed into the detention area, where a guard was waiting to show them the way. What with the expediency of Jast-Madiir's criminal justice, most of the cells they passed were empty, as usual. This, perhaps, contributed to his sudden start, when Horus heard an eerily present voice call out to him from behind the bars on his left...

"Well, hello there," Horus heard, in a quiet but commanding tone that played his spine like a xylophone. He was obliged to turn and look, and what he saw there puzzled him. "Mr. Horus Templar, isn't it?" a Meduseldan inmate inquired. "And this is undoubtedly Deborah Boulevard." He grabbed the bars between them with a couple of tentacles, while he extended yet another. "We aren't afforded many amenities here, as I'm sure you know. I don't suppose I could trouble either of you for the *time*?"

Just as Horus reached up thoughtlessly for his pocket-watch, the guard ran his nightstick along the bars with a very loud clatter, startling Horus afresh in a way that felt strangely like being roused from a dream. "Back off, you!" The guard demanded. "Stop harassing the public servants!"

The inmate floated back slowly – presented his empty tentacles innocently. "Such bad manners," he tsked. "But perhaps we'll be properly introduced yet, Mr. Templar. Wait and see."

Horus sustained a contemplative gaze, only to be gently corralled by the guard. "Don't mind him," the man urged. "It's best not to even look."

Somewhat grudgingly, they all continued. "What was that about?" Deborah asked, after they'd put a few cells between them and the mysterious inmate.

"I'm not entirely sure," Horus admitted. "But if it's what I suspect, I'm glad Art wasn't with us."

The two of them let the tense moment pass, and after just a few more cells Horus had his mind once again fixed on what lay ahead, rather than behind. His thoughts were clear, his senses tuned...

It was thus that he detected a new, unusual stimulus... a clacking sound, like ivory on concrete. He heard the same clatter a second time. A third. And, sure enough, by the time they could see the man Tweed, kneeling down on the ground of his cell, he flung a pair of dice from his cupped hands, huffing at the results... a four and a three. Horus cleared his throat...

"Excuse me, Mr. Tweed," he called.

Tweed didn't look up. He only reached out and scooped his dice back up.

"You'll remember me, of course," Horus continued.

Tweed began to shake the dice.

"I'm Horus Templar – I've been appointed to represent you."

He flung them again, still seemingly none the wiser of his visitors. A groan. A two and a five...

"...What is it you're doing, there?" Horus felt the need to ask.

"Trying to roll doubles so I can get out of this place," Tweed explained.

Horus shared a look with Deborah, just then. Her eyes radiated the message, as plain as a fifty-foot billboard: "I smell a bozo." He only nodded, and turned back...

"Arcadian..." Horus began again. "That *is* your full name, is it not? Arcadian Tweed?"

"It is," Tweed confirmed, shelving his escape efforts for the moment as he stood up. "But please, call me Bunsen Bonanza."

"I'm not going to do that," Horus replied.

Tweed shrugged. "Well, so much for formalities." He examined Horus with stern eyes, impatiently putting his hands on his hips. "What is it you want, Mr. Templar? I hope you'll make it fast. You know, you're not my favorite person in the world right now. Isn't it enough that I gave you the big finish you were hoping for to that stupid murder trial?"

Horus shook his head. "But it was never a murder trial at all! It was just a simple lawsuit."

Tweed's lips curled as he stared vehemently. "Well, if that isn't just like a tricky lawyer... luring a guy into a confession on a false pretense like that."

Horus took a moment of respite, then, rubbing the small of his head. "Listen, Arcadian..." he tried. "You may not believe it, but I'm here to help you."

"And how do you propose to do that?" Tweed huffed.

"By greasing the wheels," he explained. "You're a known killer, Arcadian. There's no changing that now. The police won't relent until they've learned everything they need to throw the book at you... whether by your own confession, or by physical evidence." He hesitated. "...They tell me you haven't been very cooperative. I'll be quite frank, Mr. Tweed... they believe you're crazy."

"Ha!" Tweed challenged. "Me, crazy? That's ridiculous! If I was crazy, could I do this?"

He proceeded to pat his head and rub his stomach at the same time... on one foot.

"More likely than not," Horus deduced.

"Well, why should I tell them anything anyway! And why should *you* of all people fault me if I'm not cooperating? You're my lawyer now... aren't you supposed to trick them into thinking I'm innocent, or something?"

It was Horus' turn to make a face. "That's *not* what I'm supposed to do. Particularly not when you've already admitted your guilt."

"Then what *can* you do?"

"I can encourage you to take the only break you're liable to get: the relative leniency the State can afford you if you make a clean breast of the whole thing. Tell us who you killed. Tell us the circumstances... the manner in which you killed him. You know, not every killing is *actually* a murder. If you killed the man on accident, that would be a lesser crime... a crime called manslaughter. But even intentional killing has degrees of severity. If you carried out some vicious, carefully-conceived plan to kill someone, that would be the most heinous thing... murder in the first degree. But if you killed in the passion of a moment – say, in a sudden burst of anger – that killing was not *premeditated*... it is only second-degree murder. So you see, you'd do much better to explain yourself... to help us rationalize what you did, the best we can. The longer you hold out, the more the State will suspect you of the highest applicable crime."

Tweed looked unconvinced. "Tell me, Mr. Templar... what is the sentence for first-degree murder?"

"Execution," Horus stated.

"...And what, pray tell, is the sentence for this manslaughter thing you're talking about?"

Horus dithered. "...Also execution," he admitted at length. "But in a less severe way."

Tweed grinned. "And I'm the crazy one?"

"Nevertheless, there's nothing more for it," Horus appealed. "You can be obstinate, but in the end you'll be found out, and you'll have earned the utmost enmity of the State for your trouble. But if you give me what they want... if you give me the *name* of the man... then things will go better for you, to the extent the law allows. So help me, Arcadian. Help me, and I'll do everything possible to help you."

Tweed shook his head. "Sounds like circular logic to me."

Horus had to turn away. The impossibility of his client had him internally screaming to storm out. He *was* crazy... apparently beyond hope of getting him to see reason...

But Horus mustered. He mastered himself, realizing that he hadn't yet exhausted his efforts. Tweed's intellect might be critically compromised... but what of his conscience? Might there be some morsel of it left that Horus could fix on? Probably not. But he had to try...

"Very well," he began, once again quite composed. "I can see you won't be persuaded to bargain for your own betterment... let alone for mine or the State's. But consider this: Neither you, nor I, nor the general welfare of this country is truly the injured party here."

Tweed searched him up and down. "What are you getting at now?"

Horus slowly drew a breath... a breath, not so much of air, as pure, righteous indignation...

"Somewhere out there, is a *man*," he explained. "That man is dead. He's dead because you killed him." His eyes made his demand for justice, as firm and fair as any words he could choose. "*Why* did you do it? Why did you kill? Can you at least tell me that?"

Tweed only turned up his palms. "Why do speckled ponies eat their own eggshells?"

Horus winced. "They don't."

"Well, there you go," Tweed summed it up. "I guess they know better than I do." He grinned an evil grin. "But then again... maybe I know just as well."

Horus whirled away in outrage. He took a big, aggressive step...

...It was all he could do to stop himself before the next one. His ears snapped sharply as he remembered one final recourse... a last weapon in his arsenal that he could try...

He turned back once more. He bored molten lasers into Tweeds eyes... he gave him *the look* again. Tweed recoiled, overwhelmed in an instant. He shut his eyes – shielded himself...

"Don't do that!" he pleaded. "Don't make that *face*! I *can't*!! I can't tell you!!"

Horus softened, feeling pity... and perhaps some regret. Such power as he apparently held was horrible to wield, even on those who most deserved it. Perhaps it was best that Tweed had reacted so quickly and averted his forcible excavation of the truth. But then, it left him still without answers. He sighed, and turned away morosely...

"Wait!" Tweed called after him.

Horus froze. He stood there, hardly looking back over his shoulder. But he did as Tweed asked. He *waited*...

"I can't give you the answer you want," Tweed said, as if earnestly apologizing. "But there is... someone else. Someone who can lead you to the one who has all the answers."

Solemnly, Horus returned to the cell. "You have my attention."

"Go to the cup booth at the Armada Inn," he explained. "Quarter of 17 sharp. Pick up the cup with the green mug handle. The password is Omnibus Nantucket. The voice on the other end will tell you what to do from there."

Horus forced himself to maintain an impassive front. This suddenly had all the earmarks of a deep, deadly conspiracy. Either that, or what was probably much more likely, his deranged new client was manufacturing sheer nonsense. But there was only one way to be sure, and that was to stick his foot right out and step in... whatever it was. Even so, he had to ask...

"This isn't just more of your absurdity, I trust?"

Tweed held up crossed fingers. "Pinky swear."

"Alright," Horus replied, despite the mixed metaphors. "I guess we'll see what turns up, in any case. Good day to you, Mr. Tweed."

"One more thing, before you go," Tweed stopped him. "I have a question for you, too. A question that's been building in my mind since I got here."

Horus nodded. "I'll answer if I can."

"What happens if I have to go to the bathroom?"

Horus blanched. He feigned looking around the corner, pointing to a spot in the back of the cell. "There's a little stall with a latrine right over there."

Tweed shook his head. "That doesn't answer my question."

This proved an impasse. Finally, Horus wrangled the best answer he could. "I would expect, the same thing as always."

Fortunately, he seemed to accept this answer. "Thank you, Mr. Templar. And good luck finding the man I killed. I almost hope you do..."

He smiled again, in the way only villains can.

"...before it's too late."

* * *

"That was bizarre," Deborah reflected aloud, the two of them fairly speeding back the way they came.

"You're very kind to put it so mildly," Horus quipped.

"If you think what he told *us* was weird, you should read Blucille's transcripts," she concluded, leafing through them. "Do us both a favor, Boss: Don't get mixed up in any more murder cases."

"I'd like to think a man like me should have such luck. But then, we still don't even know for sure if this *is* a murder case."

"Oh, it's murder. That Tweed is mad as a hatter. Why even question it? You risk sounding like you're *defending* him."

"For all express purposes, that *is* my job."

She sighed. "Don't remind me."

"Did you get all that bit about the Armada Inn and the cup booth?"

"Quarter of 17, green mug handle, Omnibus Nantucket," she recited. "It's all written out. But that's not for hours. What do we do now?"

"We report back to Blackforest, of course."

"He's not going to be a happy camper," she cautioned.

"I expect not. But it's my duty to let him know: He'll need to keep pressing on all fronts. Because until I hear a shadowy voice on the other end of that cup, I wouldn't bank on the relevance of anything Tweed's told us."

Deborah regarded him. "Do you think there's even a chance someone'll pick up?"

"I'd rather not answer that," Horus admitted. "But it has to be tried."

Before long, they made their way up to the reception room of the District Attorney's office. There was no need to engage any secretary to bring Blackforest forth. He was already lying in wait for them, arms crossed as he leaned back against a desk...

"What of it, Horus?" he asked. "Any luck?"

"Possibly a *bit* of luck," Horus replied. "But probably not much."

The DA stared daggers. "This is no time to go playing word games, Counselor. Did you get answers or didn't you?"

"I didn't," Horus admitted.

Blackforest turned around and tore a jagged hunk out of his secretary's desk with a single swipe. The room seemed rather alarmingly quiet for a while afterwards...

But finally, Horus continued...

"...However, it *is* possible he's given me a way to learn the identity of the victim."

Blackforest took a few more moments.

"...*Okay*..." he panted over his shoulder. "I guess that's a start. What can I do to help?"

"Only what you're already doing," Horus answered. "Keep exhausting every resource. I can take up the thread Tweed gave me on my own. But I have to admit... he's every bit as crazy as you made him out, Hamilton. We shouldn't make the mistake of accepting anything he tells us at face value."

"A fair point," Blackforest said, still huffing and puffing as if he'd blown a house down. "Thank you for being a steady hand in this latest calamity, Horus." He turned down to the secretary seated behind the distressed furniture. "Sorry about the mess," he told her. "Maybe I'll go and rearrange my own office for a while." Then he walked to his end of the office suite, and calmly shut the door behind him. Rather than listen for what might happen next, everyone gladly resumed their work. Blucille Cordon chose this opportune moment to return from her own office and speak with Horus herself...

"Sounds like it didn't go well," she said.

"Not especially," he replied. "Still, I'm a bit surprised how badly Hamilton took it."

"It's always a strain on him, any time the Czarina micromanages these things," she explained. "Not only that: We just received word of the High Constable's return. Which apparently means a surprise inspection of the Department."

"Goodness," Horus commiserated. "That's a lot for anyone's plate. The more I wish I could've set his mind at ease about this case."

"Did I overhear something about a *potential* lead?"

He nodded. "Tweed set me onto some caper, chasing anonymous contacts. Though of course, it's probably just a fantasy."

"Well, keep your wits about you, Templar," she warned him. "It's a fine line between crazy and crafty. Remember what happened to Art."

"I'll be careful," he affirmed.

"Any support you need, just let me know," she assured him. "We can have you tailed discreetly, if you're not sure you can handle yourself."

He laughed it off. "I doubt the need." His face turned more grave. "But perhaps there *is* something you can do for me."

"Such as?"

Horus ventured a look to be sure Blackforest was still quite shut up in his office. Even confirming he was, he proceeded quietly. "Check into Tweed's background, will you? Throw some weight around at the Embassy... find out exactly who he is and where he comes from."

Blucille looked over her own shoulder. "You know the Boss didn't want us bothering the foreign dignitaries."

"I know. But surely you recognize the folly of it, Ms. Cordon... choosing not to approach the case from all angles. If we prove unable to avail ourselves of Tweed himself, I doubt we can afford to ignore the people who know him best. Hamilton may be indisposed right now, but he'll be forced to see the need, if we don't have a breakthrough very soon. But if we show some initiative *now*, we may very well unstop this whole mystery... the thing we all need most to do."

She rested her chin on her fingers while her eyes danced across the ground. "I don't really like it," she admitted. "Going behind Blackforest's back, that is." She looked up at him. "But you're not wrong. We're hamstringing ourselves, dancing all around the Embassy."

"If you feel there's too much conflict of interest, I could just send Art," Horus offered.

It seemed then that Deborah almost spoke up about something. But only a half-syllable snuck out, and by the time they looked to her, she'd evidently changed her mind, burying her nose in her clipboard...

"No, it's alright," Blucille replied. "It'll be much faster if I handle it. I can subpoena their records; I can assign a whole team of people to the investigation."

Horus grinned. "I'd thank you to do that, Ms. Cordon. I'm sure, in time, Blackforest will thank you too."

Chapter 4

The trip back to Horus' train-car office was a quiet one. Remembering Deborah's discomfiture, he hailed a coach, and they rode most of the way. What little was said between them on the road amounted to a second, gentle invitation to lunch, which she declined graciously. Between a late breakfast and a generally spoiled appetite, she simply wasn't hungry. Horus sympathized; he wished for a way to make her feel better. But he also knew from experience that showing excessive concern would only patronize her. There was really nothing for him to do but let her work through whatever mild bug she seemed to have... and to strive for that elusive balance of thoughtful, but not *too* thoughtful. Watching her stare out the porthole of the coach, he decided a good place to start was to avoid engaging her in gratuitous conversation...

Once they reached their train, however, they found a new feature so surprising that words were inevitable...

"What in the Sam Heck?" Deborah demanded.

For his part, Horus shared her disbelief, even if he was rather alarmed at her uncharacteristically strong choice of words. "I haven't the foggiest," he replied. "Evidently, there's been some sort of mix-up." Considering the whole landscape of their private little world had been split apart by the sudden appearance of a big, brash new continent, 'mix-up' rang as somewhat of an understatement...

"Horus..." Deborah began, "...some oaf has his car wedged between our offices!"

"I'm very sure I can see that," he pointed out.

"Well of all the...!" She cut herself off. "This is just too much right now. What are we going to do about it?"

He shrugged. "What can we do but start at the start? We'll investigate."

They approached slowly, reluctantly... the way civilized people do whenever they must, in essence, find a way to politely convey the message of: 'Hello, nice to meet you, please leave.'

Perhaps it was their conspicuous sloth that drew out the proprietor of the misplaced car, leaning in their direction over his veranda's railing. Horus studied him from afar. He was a big, distinguished old Mesomela, dressed very much as Horus was, except that instead of a dark suit, his was stark white. By all appearances, the man must've been another defense attorney.

And the closer they got, the more Horus suspected he knew who. The suit itself, his general build, and the way the points of his ears drooped all added up to the caricature of one likely suspect. Then, as if to eliminate any possible doubt, Horus watched the man reach up and start to pick his teeth with the end of a broken wishbone...

"Hawdy, friends," he called from the car, once they'd reached a reasonable calling distance. He came down his boarding stairs to meet them. "Fine day we're havin', wouldn't ya say?"

"Very pleasant, yes," Horus agreed, not fully able to banish reservation from his voice. "As is the making of your acquaintance... Mr. Thalymus, I presume?" he ventured. "Nebuchadnezzar Thalymus?"

Horus watched the man's lethargic but contented features light up, confirming his suspicion. No mere oaf, they were here confronted with something of a legend in the otherwise uncelebrated annals of public defense – a courtroom maverick with a long and storied career. "Wahl, I guess ma reputation precedes me!" he said. "Right you are, Sir, yes, right you are!" He held out his hand. "But I'd be much obliged if y'd call me 'Eb'."

"Eb," Horus repeated with a nod, shaking his hand. "Glad to meet you. I'm Horus Templar."

"I thought maybe you was," Eb admitted, smiling just as if they were old friends and long-sundered. Then he turned to Deborah. "And this handsome young fille jist has ta be Deborah Boulevard!" He took her proffered hand and licked it with impeccable politeness.

"Charmed, I'm sure," Deborah replied. Meanwhile, she and Horus exchanged a brief, pained smile. Eb Thalymus was indeed a gentleman. How were they supposed to get rid of a gentleman?

"*Remarkable*," Horus stated absently, at a bit of a loss. "That this should be our first meeting, I mean. Your reputation does indeed precede you, Mr. Thalymus. You've enjoyed quite the tenure in this country."

"I 'spect thet's a polite way o' sayin' I'm old as dirt." Horus blanched, but didn't have time to work in a stammer before Eb laughed. "I like you already, Mr. Templar! I figure we'll get on like gizzard grease an' corned giblets." He pointed at Horus, looking at him sidelong. "But don't forget, now... it's *Eb*."

"My mistake," Horus said, wondering how long it was possible to smile nervously. "Of course, you may certainly call me Horus."

"Wahl then, the honor's mine, Horus. Naw, I mean that sincerely! Maybe y'ain't been around the block near so long as I have, but I don't reckon it's too early ta say: You shore is makin' a name fo' y'self."

"You're too kind," Horus replied, without so much as a trace of false modesty.

"No, naw, I can see real potential when it's starin' me straight in the face, Horus. I've had my eye on y'all for a spell. Naw, take that case with the Mantid..." He made the 'okay' gesture. "...That earned ya top marks right there. An' you've had a few gems since. But it was prob'ly the case with the Berlie Beirel as sealed the deal." He put his hands up. "It's up ta you, a'course... but I gotta hunch you're the feller I been lookin' for."

Horus cleared his throat. "This would seem to be something more than an idle crossing of paths." He ventured a look at Eb's train car. "In fact, I can't help noticing the two of us are quite suddenly on the same tracks."

Eb admired his own car, tapping it with his fist. "Wahl, I didn't wanna impose... so I brought ma own workspace. All in a day's work, hitchin' the ol' rig up. The tricky part was gettin' them ta hitch it ahead o' yours. But I figure this way – what with folks comin' ta me first – I can screen yer clients for ya. Make shore yer gettin' the cream o' the crop. I seen enough winters ta know the bad eggs from the good."

"I appreciate the thought," Horus said, interlacing his fingers. "However, I'd be remiss not to point out that Ms. Boulevard has already served admirably in that capacity." Here was the operative point. He hesitated, but came out with it. "It was *her* office just ahead of mine... until quite recently."

Eb's wide grin was undaunted. "Wahl, ain' that slick! Two screens fer the price o' one! Why, you'll have the best-vetted clients in Jast-Madiir, and no mistake!"

Horus' diplomatic front finally cracked... he frowned openly. Eb wasn't getting the picture. He would have to be more direct. "Yes, I suppose that's true. Unfortunately, there's another problem left unaddressed. You'll understand... Deborah and I are in and out of each other's offices constantly."

"No trouble a'tall!" Eb assured him. "I guarantee it won't be the *slightest* imposition. You folks is more than welcome ta barge in on me anytime! Fact, I like this better an' better! What could be more neighborly than havin' ta walk through yer neighbor's house? We'll all be thick as thieves in no time flat!"

"But..." Horus sputtered. How could he even spell it out more clearly? "But surely you see the inefficiency of it. We're working on a case right now, and we really need to..."

"Another case already?!" Eb interjected. "Well, golly-jim-coot-bobber! Why don't ya tell me all about it? Maybe I can help."

Horus wavered. "Well, I..."

"Naw, let me stop you right there," Eb coached him, hands extended in a slowing gesture. "This could be just an old feller's blatherin', but I 'spect you're makin' things too complicated, Horus. I see it with all the young bucks: always forgettin' the basics. Perhaps a simple illustration will suffice. You gotta think of a case as sorta like... well... like an *argument*. You's arguin' the one thing, an' the prosecutor, why, he's arguin' somethin' altogether differnt."

"That *is* an exceptionally simple way of looking at it," Horus admitted. "But really, Eb, I fear we're getting ahead of ourselves. Evidently you've come here with the intent of forming some sort of... professional association?"

"Right you are, Horus," he said, appearing most glad to be reminded. "Leave it ta me ta skip right over the good part! Naw let me dress it up for ya with a question... Have ya ever thought about forming a *partnership*?"

"A partnership?" Horus shrugged apologetically. "I can't say that I have."

"Wahl, that's exactly what I want ya to be thinkin' about from here out! Picture it, Horus... 'Templar & Thalymus, P.C.'! How does that grab ya?"

Horus gauged Deborah's reaction. "To tell the truth, it *is* rather catchy." He shook himself. "Even so, this really isn't the best time for..."

"...I know, I know," Eb insisted. "The case has ta come first. I respect that." He drew up alongside Horus, putting a hand on his shoulder. "In fact, why don't we all step inta yer office, so's we can hash things out a spell?"

And just like that, Horus and Deborah allowed themselves to be led by their new neighbor straight to Horus' door...

...The door with the fine monograms... as well as some fresh new marker scrawling, which – as Eb explained to Horus – was there to help him visualize the bright possibilities...

Nebuchadnezzar Thalymus & Horus Templar – Public Defenders

* * *

For a span of time far exceeding anything his pocket watch would care to chronicle, Horus allowed himself to be the target of Eb's typhoon of exposition, which he'd evidently spent the last hundred years in the field carefully snowballing for just such an occasion. He even made an honest effort to listen for the first half hour or so. But after all, an experienced attorney could only take so much lecturing about fundamentals. Actually, even 'fundamentals' seemed a generous term. It was clear from the earliest that Eb had a panache for relating ideas so basic that even the layman would have trouble not letting his eyes glaze over. It didn't help that the old fellow's voice was about as energizing as a swirling spiral of honey and molasses. To hear him go on and on without interruption was tantamount to imbibing the world's most perfect sedative. Between bouts of what could've been described as fully upright narcolepsy, Horus goaded himself back to consciousness just enough to discover that Eb sometimes meandered into such stimulating topics as food, the weather, and the fit of different cummerbunds he'd owned...

Through it all, Horus was distantly aware that Deborah had planted herself by the window. His eyes often settled on her still looking out on the world, even if his mind was really elsewhere... a place that strongly resembled a continuous state of being tucked into bed. Such was the torpor inside Horus' car that when, at last, Deborah stepped away from the pane, it had about the effect of a bomb going off...

"What is it?!" Horus demanded with bated breath. No development was too small right now to be exciting.

"Art's here," she said.

"Art?" Eb asked. "Who's Art?"

"He's a friend – a private investigator." Horus shot up. "We'd better go meet him..."

"No, that's alright," Deborah waved him down, already miles ahead and halfway through the door. "I'll see what he wants. The two of you can go on talking."

Horus gaped. He could *never* have imagined such betrayal at the hands of his otherwise superlative secretary! But there was nothing for it. She closed the door and was gone...

"A fine secretary indeed, that Ms. Boulevard," Eb remarked. "I can see she's owed all her acclaim."

"Yes," Horus nodded. "She does her job well. Perhaps *too* well."

Eb groaned as he settled his old bones back into his seat. "Naw, back to brass tacks. Where were we?"

* * *

Hands in the pockets of his trench coat and eyes trained sullenly on the ground in true, hardboiled gumshoe fashion, Art drew up on Horus' car with autonomous precision. Even with recent memory loss issues, this route was so mindless by now that he almost noted too late the strange new car in the train. It gave him pause. But before he could long contemplate this mystery, Deborah surprised him again as she came running up to him...

"Debs," he said, pointing past her. "There's a big ol' railcar right behind your office. And it's not Horus'."

She sighed. "Yes, Art. Thanks for doing the detective bit and being so quick to notice."

He grinned. "Sure thing. In my line of work, it's best not to take the big obvious details for granted." He squinted, searching further down the line. "Oh good, I see Horus is in. Who's the old guy?"

"The owner of the big ol' railcar: Eb Thalymus."

"*Nebuchadnezzar* Thalymus?!" Art exclaimed. "Boy, a real somebody! I better go introduce myself..."

Deborah stopped him. "Maybe some other time. The way things are going, you might have plenty of opportunities." She looked at him seriously. "Right now, there's something that demands your attention."

Art nodded. "I got a message from Horus... some job he wanted to talk to me about. That's why I'm here."

"*I* sent that message," she explained. "There's a job *I* need to talk to you about. Privately."

* * *

Art seated himself in Deborah's office, watching her bolt doors and check up and down through her windows on both sides. It certainly seemed she had a mind to be discreet. Finally, once she was satisfied their conversation was secure, she sat opposite him, searching his eyes intently. None of this was strictly ordinary behavior for Deborah, and it left Art a bit stymied...

"Well, here we are," he pointed out meekly. "What's shakin', Debs?"

"We'll get to that in a moment," she replied. "First I have something to ask *you*. Did you mean what you said, back at Civil HQ? About the Syzygy?"

"You mean, do I think terrible things are gonna happen because the planets are lining up?" He shrugged. "Sure. Maybe."

Deborah sighed again. "I guess that'll have to be good enough." She pointed very accusingly in his face. "What I'm about to tell you does *not* leave this room."

Art fearfully lifted his right hand. "Scout's honor."

"Good," she nodded forcefully.

For a while afterwards, they both sat silently... Art doing his best to prepare for whatever she was about to say, even as she stared at him on and on... with apparently less and less disposition to say anything at all.

"Well?" he managed to ask at length. "What is it?"

"Oh, *fusspots*!" she exclaimed, turning away from him. She threw her hands up. "Now I don't even know if I can tell you! No matter how I try, it's going to come out sounding so stupid!"

"Stupid I can handle," he assured her. "Lay it on me, sister."

"*Alright*," she intoned, nervously snickering. "But I'm telling you, this is a real doozy."

"Understood."

"If you laugh, I might have to slap you."

"Duly noted."

She drew in a big breath, choosing a handy window to look distantly through. She rubbed the fur on the back of her neck. And then, she began...

"These last few nights..." she faltered. "Well, there've been... *symptoms*. I don't see so well in the dark. I can hardly smell anything. My feet are swollen and it's all I can do to get them in my shoes. I'm getting bald patches on my elbows. The sight, the taste... even the *thought* of decent food turns my stomach!"

Art made quick use of his notepad. "Okay. Sounds pretty rough. But here's the thing: I'm a private eye, not a doctor. Don't you think you should be talkin' to one of those instead?"

She shook her head. "Not if this all adds up to what I think it does. What I'm *afraid* it does..."

"Which is?"

She struggled, being put to the question again. "I think... possibly... what with the Syzygy and all..." It was all she could do to push through. "I think I might be turning into a Werehuman."

Art about dropped his notepad. "A Werehuman? No kidding?"

"Believe me, I wish I was."

He suddenly bobbed in his chair, gesturing excitedly. "Well, come on then: Let's see the trick! Do the transforming number! I'm not scared!"

"It doesn't work like that, Art!" she replied, putting her hands on her hips. "Sure, there are lingering effects, but the transformation only happens when I'm asleep. Or anyway, that's what I was always told."

His enthusiasm rapidly deflated. "So then, you really don't know for sure if you're turning into one of those... those *things*?"

"Why do you think I'm hiring *you*?" she rejoined. "I'm afraid to know the answer... more afraid than I'd like to admit. But the evidence is stacking up... I can't afford to ignore it."

"Still sounds to me like something to take up at the doctor's office," Art reiterated. "Those are some wacky symptoms, but there could be all kinds of explanations. You might just be sick. Or..." Suddenly, he experienced a flash of memories... distant memories of some of his mother's complaints, about the time she was going to have his second round of brothers and sisters. "Well..." he said delicately, not entirely convinced this was a wise question to venture. "...Do you think it's possible you're just... you know..." He squeaked out what remained. "...On the nest?"

Her eyes gorged with incendiary outrage. "Artimus Mallard!" she huffed. "Why, of all the hair-brained questions in the world! How could I *possibly* be *pregnant*?! You know I don't have a husband!"

"But I *didn't* know!" he shouted back, recoiling. "That is, you could've had one and I just forgot about him!" He pointed at his head. "I'm still running into those memory lapses once in a while, ya know!"

Fortunately, her look softened. She seemed suddenly frail, collapsing into one of her own chairs. "You're right. I'm sorry, Art. You're just trying your best to help me eliminate the impossible. But you need to understand: I have good reason to suspect what I do. I know to most people, 'Werehumans' are just silly, baseless myths. But *you* try waking up every morning, drenched head-to-toe in a pool of cold sweat, and see if you don't start to wonder if maybe there's some credence to it all."

Art's face bunched up quizzically. "Waking up in a cold sweat? That's not so weird."

"Well, don't forget: We only sweat with our tongues."

Art blanched. "You got me there."

"And besides," she continued hauntingly, "I've been warned – ever since I was a little girl – it's in my family's blood."

"Not a great-grandfather on your mother's side, I hope?" he inquired, knowing something of the folklore.

Her frown expanded, and she nodded. "'Fraid so. I never saw him turn for myself, mind you. But I know great-grandma used to bolt him in the cellar every time two planets even got close to each other."

"Yikes."

"Oh Art, it's been so horrible!" she lamented. "I haven't even told you the worst part yet!"

He sighed. "Well, no sense stopping short now... let's have it all."

"A few nights ago, I had some especially awful fever-dreams. I woke up feeling really bloated... like I'd overeaten. And then... then I got the paper..."

"What about it?"

"There was a story. A man was eaten right out of his shoes... just outside the Sauropod Street Zoo."

"...Yeah?"

"Well, don't you see!" she demanded. "Art, that zoo is only a few blocks from my *house*!"

The conclusion stopped him up. But once again, he didn't find himself deeply concerned. "You... you think you mighta ate a guy?"

"That's what I'm most afraid of, yes," she admitted with great pain.

He almost laughed. "Debs, I've known you a long time," he reminded her endearingly. "You would never eat a Human. Particularly if you were turning into one."

She got indignant again. "But I'm **not** turning into a Human. I'm turning into a *Werehuman*! I need you to try and appreciate the difference."

"What exactly is the difference?" he asked.

She turned out her hands in utter exasperation. "*I don't know*!!"

At this point, he stood up – crossed the room. He patted her on the shoulder reassuringly. "I'll look into it for ya. The death you're talking about wasn't listed as suspicious by the SAPD, what with the things they keep in the zoo, and all. But if anyone asks, I can make it seem like I'm there for the Tweed killing."

She smiled weakly at him. "Thanks, Art. It means a lot."

He packed up his notepad, mustering resolution to say more. "In the meantime, I think you should talk about this with Horus. You're important to him, Deborah... he's bound to notice if you're wound this tight, sooner or later. The truth's the best remedy."

She shook her head. "I can't do that. I could never admit to... to believing I've been turning into a hideous, disgusting monster. Not to *him*." There was a wistful look in her eye just then, it seemed. "Horus is a very dignified man,

Art. His mind is logical... well-ordered. You're the only one I can trust with this."

"Think about it," he urged her with one final pat. Then he stood up. "But I'll let you know what I learn, soon as I can."

"Please do. I won't be able to sleep until I know. Or anyway, even if I could, it wouldn't be very responsible."

He winked at her. "Don't worry your little head, Debs. I'm sure you're right as rain. You'll see."

Chapter 5

I hope she really didn't eat a guy, Art mused to himself, enroute to the Sauropod Street Zoo. He wasn't entirely sure why he had any doubt. Maybe it was just the way that telling ladies not to worry their little heads had tended to herald disaster in the past. Maybe it was the distant, oblong outline of four Other Worlds slowly converging overhead, fairly pointing his way to the zoo – even in broad daylight – that left him ill at ease. Or, maybe he was just a bit of a pessimist by nature. Yes, as a hardboiled gumshoe, that was probably it.

Before long, he found himself at the front gate of one of St. Argonsburg's most infamous attractions. He studied a big, mural-style billboard emblazoned with the image of a buggy-eyed man in a black turtleneck. It read, in huge letters: "SAUROPOD STREET ZOO: DEEPLY REVILED AND PUBLICLY DECRIED BY WORLD-RENOWNED THINKER ZEPH BRONZEGLOOM!!!". Then, he turned his eyes up to the sign directly over the large wooden gateway: a silhouette of a brachiosaur sauntering down a paved road. *Dinosaurs...* Art reflected. *What a boring theme for a zoo!* He could hardly help flipping to a new page in his notepad and recording a wild idea that struck him out of the blue. *What about a zoo filled with smallish mammals that were docile enough that you could walk right up and touch them? Man, that would be far out...*

No sooner than he finished jotting, and a big, surly, crusty, and generally scarred-over Human came over and greeted him. "Got a ticket, buster?"

"Nope," Art replied. "I'm no tourist. I'm a detective, here on vaguely police-ish business."

The large man sighed. "This about the shoe guy?"

"You got it. I'd like to speak with a manager. And I'd like to be shown the scene of the crime." He caught himself. "Or, well, the scene of where the eating that's hopefully *not* a crime happened." He caught himself again, remembering that his whole cover-story was to pretend he was investigating a possible Tweed victim. "That is, the scene of the *presumed* eating that may or may not be connected to a crime we're investigating."

"I'll get you a manager," the man muttered before turning away.

* * *

Art sat himself at a bench just inside the zoo while he waited. There were beautiful flamingos and ducks aplenty to admire in ponds all around the landing area that branched into the many taxonomies on display. A quick perusal of the map had revealed: There were deadly large assortments of birds, reptiles, insects, and mammals, giant killer dinosaurs and sea titans, all the way up to eldritch monstrosities that tended to defy tidy classification, such as hydras and mandrakes and junk...

But while other folks' minds might've freely wandered down those paths, or simply appreciated the placid birds in the little pools, Art engaged himself in people-watching. He was especially fond of watching mothers and fathers try to wrangle their little kids, who for fear of their lives demonstrated great resistance to being hauled beyond the landing. It was a common scene. Sure, the zoo was advertised as a fun and frivolous exhibition, for those who had time for such things. But most Jast-Madiirans who made the pilgrimage to a zoo did so as a sort of rite in child-rearing. There simply wasn't a handier way to inspire healthy fear in young minds than to go down paths of wall-to-wall cages, point to enormous feral beasts inside, and say: 'Look, Little Jimmy. Look at all the things in the world that can kill you.'

For their part, the children seemed to have some appreciation for the spirit in which they'd been brought here. Art enjoyed a special chuckle, watching one little guy kick and flail as his dad fireman-carried him down the sea-monster path. "*Kids,*" he doted aloud to himself. "What a bunch a' wimps."

CRUNCH

A huge foot with claws like obsidian scimitars stomped the cobblestone directly beside Art, causing his seated body to achieve spontaneous vertical motion as he yelped like a little girl. He turned and looked up... and *up*... into shifting eyes filled with poison-neon hues around bilaterally slitted pupils, heralded by a long, serrated snout full of fangs he could've used to scale a cliff face. And before he could make a move... let alone remember what moving was... the jaws of that snout opened up...

"Welcome to Sauropod Street Zoo," the jaws said pleasantly. "You're the detective, I take it?"

"W... well yes," Art replied, swimming through the wash of adrenaline as he slowly began to compose himself. "Artimus Mallard's the name. You... must be the *manager*?"

"Indeed!" the jaws replied as they nodded with tree-snapping force. "I am Balchikahn, and pleased to make your acquaintance." He lifted gaunt, scaly knuckles wrapped in folds of leathery sails from the ground to gingerly shake Art's tiny hand.

"Nice to meet you too, Balchikahn," Art said as they shook. But he suddenly felt the weight of a faux pas. "Sorry if I kinda lost my cool there, for a second. Nothing personal."

"Don't trouble yourself about it, Mr. Mallard," Balchikhan assuaged him. "You're here investigating an eaten man, and I – a huge carnivorous lizard – fairly got the drop on you, it seems. Context is everything! Anyway, I am rather accustomed to being mistaken for a part of this menagerie by now." He leaned back into a more upright stance, running a clawed hand through tassels hanging from his head and down a vibrant vest. "I try to dress ostentatiously in the hopes of appearing quite as sapient as possible." He shrugged. "But even so, I must always concede – the sight of a civilian Avarican is passing abnormal."

Art nodded. "Particularly one of your size. What are you on, now... if you don't mind my asking? Fourth life? Fifth?"

"You have it at fifth, my good man," the manager answered.

"Well, how about that? You're lookin' pretty trim and clear-eyed for a fiver, I'd say," Art complimented, as if he would know. But he'd found being conversational was always a good way to go. "I can imagine it's easy to run up the count in your line of work here."

Here, Art might've erred. For a face that was clearly designed to kill anyway, Balchikhan's features suddenly seemed to contort in a way that looked slightly miffed. "I beg your pardon, Mr. Mallard," he growled haughtily. "I would have you know that I run an *exceptionally* safe zoo, with fewer than a dozen incidents of patron consumption per year! Granted, you have come with regard to one such incident. And – as you are bound to learn very soon from your examination anyway – I must admit that there are... well... a *few* of our animals whose exact whereabouts are currently shrouded in some level of uncertainty. But I assure you, our caution in managing these creatures is unrivaled – our safety record is unimpugnable – and there is no clear and present reason that you should insinuate otherwise."

Without even really meaning to, Art's gaze wandered down to Balchikhan's other arm... particularly, the half of it that was missing.

"...It was lost in a traffic accident," Balchikhan claimed as he turned and cradled his stump.

Art shrugged. "Your story, pal. I didn't mean anything by it. Just figured it probably helps to be on par with some of the beasties around here. A dinosaur handling dinosaurs, so to speak."

"True enough," he nodded. "In fact, it was very much in the vein of that reasoning that I sought this appointment in the first place. I have always meant that my work should be virtuous, sparing those less physically impressive than myself from excessive peril. I aspire to the highest standards of model citizenship." He slouched a bit, though his upper body already hunched naturally under its own bulk. "Still, I have my *detractors*..."

"The Inquisition give you a hard time?" Art ventured.

Balchikhan leaned in. "They watch me *constantly*."

"Eh, I'm sure it's not as bad as ya think," Art waved it off.

Balchikhan looked off to his right, and Art's eyes traced his gaze to a bench across the landing area. There sat an Inquisitor, who – upon being observed – slowly buried his masked face in the newspaper he was holding.

"Okay, so maybe it is."

"The nerve of it!" Balchikhan dratted in a low voice. "You'd think a lifetime of good behavior would count for something – particularly a lifetime of a few hundred years. *Ha*! As if I would make mischief the moment they turn their backs!" He eyed Art seriously. "Do you know, I hardly even think about my treasure?"

"I believe you," Art went along.

"Though, it is very shiny."

Art shrugged. "Probably is."

"And comfortable! I never truly knew what sleep was until that first night I had a pile of copper shillings to rest my head on!"

"Uh-huh."

He raised his hand to his chin as he looked pensively into the distance. "However, I do find myself wondering of late what I might do to keep it a little better hidden..."

"*Oh*-kay!" Art stopped him. "You're digging yourself into a bit of a hole here, Pal. Maybe we oughta move on to something else."

Balchikhan turned back to him. "Agreed. Never mind the troubles of a gentle giant – ever the object of unfair presumption," he lamented. "You have sought me out, and here I am. How can I be of aid in your investigation, Mr. Mallard?"

Art's ears snapped taut as he refocused. "I want you to show me the place where the guy got ate. The spot where the shoes were found."

The manager nodded. "I can do that, easily enough. Or, perhaps I can do one better."

"Like what?"

"I can show you the *shoes*."

* * *

"All publicity is good publicity… or so the Board of Directors would have me believe," Balchikhan explained, leading Art under a long, dark portico. "Would that we could promote ourselves for what we truly are – an exemplar of safety among zoos! Instead, we have taken to magnifying every small scandal."

"I did note the billboard out front," Art replied. "You don't often see 'decried' and 'deeply reviled' in advertising."

"That's a perfect example of what I mean," Balchikhan nodded. "Zeph Bronzegloom was invited to tour this facility shortly before its public opening, along with a lawyer and a few scientists and small children, as is customary. But of all their opinions of the place, his was the most scalding by far. I grant that he also commanded orders of magnitude more celebrity than the rest of the guests, and that must account for something. Still, I feel as if the Directors would've been sorely displeased, if the man had actually found the place to his liking."

"Where's the logic in that?" Art asked. "If there *is* any, it's lost on me."

Balchikahn shrugged as he pushed through a doorway that barely accommodated him. "Notoriety breeds curiosity, I suppose. Hence the display hall we keep here."

Art searched down the hall, finding it full of skylights falling on a long row of short pillars. Each pillar had some unremarkable little trinket on it in a glass case. He drew up on the first one, squinting as he tried to find a way to attach any significance to what he was looking at…

"Okay Balchikhan, ya got me…" he admitted. "Why am I looking at half a pencil and a roughed-up notebook?"

"Why don't you read the last entry? That ought to prove revealing."

Art obliged, pressing the length of his nose up against the glass. "Sauropod Street Zoo… tasteless entryway… boring flamingos… walkways too narrow… Carnotaurus out of its caaaaa------." Art paused. "It ends there with a big lead streak."

Balchikhan nodded. "It was actually a Saurophaganax, but to be fair, the two are often confused."

"So then, this was left behind by somebody who came for the zoo, but stayed for dinner?"

"Yes. We learned later that he was a journalist, sent here for an interest piece. Based on these notes, they actually published his story posthumously: 'Sauropod Street Zoo Fails to Meet Expectations.'"

Art pointed to the next display. "What about this one?"

"The hat of a newsman who came here to sate his curiosity about an exotic sandworm. He had a closer look than he bargained for."

"So this entire hall is a showcase for that notoriety/curiosity dynamic you were talking about," Art surmised.

"It is indeed," Balchikhan confirmed. "The last earthly trinkets of those unfortunate few who fall victim to minor containment abnormalities are curated and displayed here." He pointed down the row. "There is the handkerchief of a man who was instantaneously dissolved by the acid-snot of a salamander... a specially grim irony, I would say. And beyond that, the wristwatch of a man swallowed by anaconda snake."

"...And at the end, the shoes of our latest poor sap, no doubt," Art determined. His jowls suddenly scrunched up. "How do you wiggle out of a wristwatch while you're being swallowed whole?"

"Who can say?" Balchikhan replied. "In any event, you are correct. The shoes in question were put on display this very morning."

Art's eyes ventured all the way to the last little pillar, hardly spying it through a dense gathering of people. "Evidently they haven't been overlooked."

The manager sighed. "No, they haven't. They never are. The Directors must be given this: Their parade of little horrors does attract a lot of attention... more than the animals themselves, it often seems. We boast the world's only Kraken living in captivity, yet the people come to gawk at a pair of loafers. But come – let us see them for ourselves."

* * *

"So what do you know about this fella?" Art asked as Balchikhan carefully removed the glass case. "*Something*, I assume. You seemed to know plenty about the rest."

"His name was Grigori, I am told. They found his shoes on the sidewalk, just beyond the west wall of the zoo. Evidently, something intercepted him there, on his nightly walk home from the presses."

"The *presses*?" Art repeated. "As in, newspaper?"

"Correct," Balchikhan confirmed.

Art's face curdled in disbelief. "You mean to tell me he was *another* journalist?"

Balchikhan only nodded. "The overwhelming majority of victims in these incidents have been journalists by trade. That is why you will never get me to believe that animals do not have discerning tastes."

Art nodded in return even as he grimaced, vaguely troubled that to some extent, he shared Balchikhan's sentiment. Though the reasons eluded most people, it was universally understood: Journalists were iffy, at best...

"I see," Art rejoined. "But you *are* convinced he was eaten?"

"I am *confident*, to be sure," Balchikhan answered, sounding rather the opposite.

"I don't suppose you'd happen to know by *what*, exactly?" Art's own confidence was beginning to dwindle. It seemed this Grigori had indeed been eaten *outside* of the zoo proper, just as Deborah said. And not only that, he'd been eaten on the side closest to her house! Art sincerely hoped Balchikhan could prove that some creature of his own was responsible. He held his breath for any kind of confirmation...

"I'm afraid not," the manager admitted. "As I earlier indicated, there are *a few* of our animals which could conceivably be on the lam. A tiger... a Dilophosaurus... a Jabberwock... a moose..."

"Mooses don't eat people," Art stated confidently.

"May it be as you say, Mr. Mallard," Balchikhan shrugged. "Given the temperament of the ones who reside here, I could never be sure."

Art folded his arms, reaching up to cradle his fuzzy chin as he mused. "At any rate, there's no smoking gun," he lamented. "That's a far cry from what I wanted to hear."

Balchikhan cast his gaze down, obviously waxing uncomfortable. "If I may be so bold, Sir... do you suppose that I might inquire something of *you*?"

"You just did," Art said, ever of the quick wit to point out when he was being asked to answer a question. "But sure, go ahead."

"Well..." the manager hesitated... "I do wonder what it is that's inspired your visit? The police investigation was open and shut. Now a detective comes for a second look... gauges my conviction that the man was indeed consumed by roving beast. Could it be that... I mean... do you hope to rule-out some *other* explanation for Mr. Grigori's expiry?"

Art nodded rather absently as he looked at the shoes. "That *is* what I hope to do."

"Then it must be as I feared," Balchikhan said, grave and ominous.

Art straightened back up, confused. "What do you mean?"

"Well, there is no mistaking the obvious extrapolation of the facts, Mr. Mallard. You simply *must* be here to examine this man's candidacy as the victim of the *Syzygy Killer*." The huge Avarican managed to put just the right sensational emphasis on the last two words...

"The Syzygy Killer?" Art questioned.

"Yes. The alias and alter-ego of a one Arcadian Tweed. It's in all the papers..." Naturally, Balchikhan had such a paper handy, and produced it for Art's benefit...

"Arcadian Tweed Dubbed Syzygy Killer," Art recited, getting a bad taste in his mouth. "'Dubbed' by who?"

"Such a question! Who would think to ask? There is no answer. He simply *is* dubbed!" Balchikhan reached for yet another paper. "Here's a more recent one."

"Syzygy Killer Threatens City – May Be Released at Conjunction." Art shook his head. "Boy, they're really pushing this one."

"Can they really be faulted, in such a case?" Balchikhan asked. "I understand the administration has little regard for the lives of the general peasantry... that is only right and proper. But to willfully unleash a manic killer on us, at such a troubling time? I fail to see how that does anything for law and order. It has a senselessness about it... almost a *madness*. It's enough to make anyone wonder... what further weirdness awaits us, as the Syzygy progresses? What uncanniness? What *terrors*?"

"You've got this all wrong," Art contested. He waved the paper in his hand. "You're letting these fancy headlines and your own imagination lead you 'round the bend! Tweed's release has nothing at all to do with the Syzygy. They just can't hold him indefinitely without evidence."

"But it *is* true, then?" Balchikhan pressed him anxiously. "You're an agent in this Tweed investigation? You've come in regard to it?"

Here, Art was at a loss. He'd given Deborah his assurance that he'd use Tweed as a cover in a pinch... but that was before he had any appreciation for the broader implications...

"I... I can't really say that I haven't," he explained. He felt a sudden pang. "...But I can't really say that I *have*, either..."

Balchikhan's banded irises searched him intently. "I see," he commented at length. He turned to indicate the shoes. "Either way, here is your evidence. I do hope something good can come of their study."

"You and me both, Pal." And with that, he resumed his scrutiny...

Visually, there was nothing remarkable about either shoe. No external damage or discoloration. They were the slip-in kind, which surely accounted for how the man was able to slip out of them in his last moments. But that was about the extent of what Art could learn with his eyes. Thankfully, he had other resources...

WHIFFFFF, he sniffed. The results were not pleasant, but they *were* revealing...

"Yup," Art announced, before running a confirmation check with a second probe of olfactory data. "There's a whopper of a sweat stink, but I definitely smell a little drool in there, too."

"Ah, very clever, Mr. Mallard... yes, most concrete. It's a wonder the policemen who came before you didn't think to try it!"

Art pointed at his nose. "It's all about having the right equipment." He grimaced as he struck a posture of rumination. "Still, that's half a job, at best. We thought he was eaten before. Now we *know*. But by what?"

Seemingly on cue, his eyes strayed up to the crowd of gawkers, who had silently obliged them with a wide berth from the moment he and Balchikhan had approached the shoe display, for whatever reason. He snapped his clawed fingers, seeing he had what he needed to complete his investigation close at hand...

Purposefully, he walked right up to a guy...

"Hey, you," he politely engaged the midsize Human. "Could you open your mouth for a sec?"

"Um..." the man replied thoughtfully. But finally, he shrugged. "Okay." He hesitantly obliged.

WHIF-WHIF, went Art's nose, assimilating copious information. "Alright, good." He leaned back upright, finding the initial examination hopeful, but recognizing a need to establish a reliable baseline. He turned to a nearby Human woman. "Okay, now you."

He proceeded to sniff her breath, and that of two other people, before Balchikhan could help himself no longer...

"Pardon me again, Sir... what is it you're presently engaged in?"

"I need to be sure exactly what Human drool smells like," Art explained. He didn't have time to regret his frankness, before the zoo's manager continued...

"You... you don't suppose it's actually possible that... that it was *Mr. Tweed* who ate Grigori!"

Art blanched... his dark eyes bugging all the way to the whites. "No, *no*! I mean... well... certainly not! But it doesn't hurt to... what I mean is..."

"Good heavens!" Balchikhan interjected, the color draining from his sandy-colored scales. "The Syzygy Killer... a *cannibal*! I... I may faint..."

"No, it's alright, Balchikhan, really!" Art assured him amidst the growing murmur of the Humans, catching himself in the middle of a dash to steady the huge manager... realizing that if he tried, he'd only get pancaked for his trouble. "The drool on the shoes doesn't match the smell of their breath! We're in the clear!" Privately, he was very glad. He'd confirmed his friend's good name! But now, he could only hope he hadn't accidentally frazzled anyone too much in the process...

"Oh, *thank the Creators*," Balchikhan heaved, sinking to a very heavy sit. "To imagine a killer in our midst was bad enough! But if I had known the true extent of your suspicions..."

"It's not that I suspected Tweed of eating people," Art tried. "You gotta believe me on that. But my work here wouldn't've been done if I wasn't *absolutely sure*." He turned his hands up. "There's nothing more to it, I promise."

"If you say so, Mr. Mallard," a weak Balchikhan replied. "Still, I am *shaken*. Even at the height of my people's savagery, we did not joyfully *eat* other intelligent creatures. We certainly did not eat our *own*!" He had a very shell-shocked look about him. "What a wretched thing. Dreadful..."

Seeing he wouldn't collapse, Art came over and patted him. "Cheer up, Buddy. It didn't go down that way. Tweed's no cannibal. Just your garden-variety psychotic killer."

"I will endeavour to take your word for it," he said, collecting himself... standing back up and brushing off. "Anyway, it would seem we're right back where we started... the search for the missing animals must go on now. At least one of them has certainly escaped." He warmed the air with a sigh. "I only hope it was not the Jabberwock... of all our beasts, it is by far the most frumious." Even as he recounted these things to himself, he finally turned to Art. "I don't suppose, Mr. Mallard, that we might enlist your help, pinpointing the culprit?"

Art shook his head. “Sorry, Mac... my work here is done. Makes no difference who did it, as long as I know who *didn’t* do it.” He slid his ears into his chic little detective hat as he reached into a pocket in his trench coat. “Of course, you’re at liberty to hire me yourself. Here’s my card. Just know I don’t work cheap. Especially not when it means sniffing monster breath.”

Chapter 6

"An' ya know, the work can get right thankless at times," Eb droned on, having shown no obvious concern over the last several hours with whether the cataleptic Horus could hear him any longer or not. "I've had clients TP ma house, bust up ma mailbox... Why, I even had one little lady splash me with red grape juice, all over ma best white blazer! Course, I 'spect she meant nothin' by it... 'cept that she was offended somethin' fierce by ma very existence. But naw that's jist the culture! You gotta be prepared fo that! You gotta *roll* with them punches! You gotta look yer client straight in the eye an' say, 'I's gonna help you, no matter how much ya hate me fo it!' You gotta..."

Just then, the door opened, jumpstarting Horus' dusty neurons. Deborah leaned in solemnly from the gathering dusk.

"It's time," she said.

* * *

The dark of night settled on St. Argonsburg, overtaking Horus enroute to the Armada Inn. Everywhere the mood was tense... quietly discordant. Everything felt a little off. The never-ending maze of streetlamps cast their quivering pools of light into a pallor of restless blue shadows, rendered in unusual hues that read like a forgery. Few things Horus could spy were truly black... and those that were seemed blacker than usual...

But what he really noted was the soundscape. Mostly, he noted its relative absence. Surely, at no point in the history of a metropolis had a night been so muted as this one. Even here – down by the coast – he more than half believed he could hear his train marching slowly up the tracks of Mt. Norvein, some miles now behind him. Though he passed Human commuters on every side, their shuffling feet were so light on the ground tonight that he wondered if they even touched the cobblestone...

For their part, the people almost seemed to be wondering the same thing... if the way they kept their eyes locked down was any clue. Discretion had prompted Horus to don a jazz cap and a long overcoat, as if to pass himself off as an investigator. But no one saw his hat... his face. Few would've even seen his coattails. Everywhere he looked, his were the only eyes to stray an inch above the beaten path. He couldn't figure it out – this sudden, universal determination to avoid looking up. Had he missed some new edict? No... Deborah would've made sure of that. Something *else*... something altogether mysterious was going on...

Whatever it was, he'd have to get to the bottom of it later. There was presently another mystery that demanded his full attention. He was dressed as a detective, and in a way – for tonight, at least – he *was*. He had to admit a palpable electricity about it... the daring, the intrigue. Never mind how little stock he'd initially put in this game of cat and mouse Tweed had set him on. Cursory research earlier that day had revealed there *was* an Armada Inn, and it *had* a cup booth. That gave this errand at least some basis in fact.

But beyond any rationale he might point to, Horus could feel his instincts glowing orange-hot. There was a distinct sense of anticipation in the air... whether for better or worse. That pretty much summed-up his mood... and the people's as well...

At last, he reached the Inn. For a healthy interval, he stood across the street from it, just taking in the scene, feeling confident that's what Art would do in his place. He consulted his watch. Then, even seeing he'd arrived in plenty of time, he sucked in his gut and took the plunge...

"Hello, Sir," a man at the desk called out. Horus was glad to be noticed by the staff... apparently, whatever had everyone looking down didn't apply so much indoors. "Can I interest you in our most deluxe amenities? We have plenty of rooms available."

"Not tonight, I'm afraid," Horus replied, leaning over the counter. "I'm just here for the cup booth," he quietly explained.

The man sighed. "Of course." He pointed off to his right. "The booths are there, just beyond the archway. Flat rate of ten shillings per call, not to exceed one minute in length."

Horus fished through his change, looking seriously as he set ten coins on the board. "There's one other thing. I have to place the call at a set time. Is there someplace I can wait where I won't be in the way?"

The man persisted in his tired air. "New to the game of espionage, are we? You may join the others, sitting all about the lobby."

"Thank you," Horus nodded.

Sure enough, when he turned back to sit down, he noticed for the first time that there were over a dozen men in dark hats and coats already seated in the room. As he took his place among them, he felt silly that he hadn't anticipated a scene like this. He did, after all, have cursory knowledge of cup-calls. They were certainly an interesting innovation, noted for taking simple, everyday cups and twine and turning them into the means of opening the bold new frontier of telecommunications. However, seeing as a call could only span the length of string between cups on both ends, the application of the technology was rather limited. Places with cup booths were, at best, wired into other places with cup booths a door or two down the road. Most of the time, calls never even left the building, with strings simply running from one individual booth to another, as was the case here. That tended to limit the clientele of cup-callers to two main categories: people with money to burn on childish novelties, and people looking for a theatrical means to trade fringe information they probably had no business knowing in the first place. Judging by the prevalence of high collars and low hats in the room, not to mention the powerful whiff of pipe-soap he was picking up on, Horus had a pretty good idea which category predominated the night...

The quiet wait for 16:45 whiled by anxiously. Horus spent much of the time trying to sneak peaks at the obscured faces around him. Any one of them could be the man on the other end of the call he was here to place. Or, maybe that man wasn't here yet. Maybe he was already waiting in the next room. Maybe he didn't exist and had never existed. Horus agonized for some clue – any clue at all. But there was none to be had...

Even so, the time to act eventually came. At the stroke of 16:44, Horus stood up and made his way into the next room, brushing past shifty characters coming and going. Catching sight of the first few booths in the row, he felt a flash of anxiety. He needed to find the cup with the green mug handle. He'd given himself only a minute to find it and make his call. And of course, he couldn't be sure the booth in question wasn't already occupied... if in fact there was such a booth at all. It was rather a lot of ifs and uncertainties to juggle all at once...

But in this much, he needn't have worried. Coming up on Booth 4, he found his quarry – green handle and all – unoccupied. He slid the sound-proof glass door open, even as he made one last scan of the room for shadowy eyes that might be on him. Nothing stuck out. He closed the door behind him and turned to the cup station...

All sound but his own breath banished, the already-small space seemed instantly to shrink while his gaze danced over the rudimentary console, almost pressed into his stout stomach. There was little to see... only the cup on its hook, with its string running up into the box. And over that, he found a small marquee set behind glass...

"14"

He grabbed his chin, musing. The booths were all numbered. This marquee must've indicated which booth his cup was strung to. That was information he could use. He might yet get his chance to confront Tweed's contact face-to-face...

He slowly picked up the cup. He set it against his ear. He bent full concentration into his sharp sense of sound, straining to detect even the slightest shift on the other end of the string...

Nothing. Nothing but the constant roar of the ocean. He almost suffocated himself, trying not to make the slightest noise of his own. Finally – begrudgingly – he took a moment to produce his watch. The seconds ticked loudly, slowly by...

At last, his powers of rationality prevailed on his instincts. *What am I doing here*? he wondered. *Why did I believe Tweed's nonsense for a second? Did I really think that he would...*

And suddenly, there it was... be it ever so faintly: a rustling sound on the other end of the line. He checked his watch: only a second past 16:45. He heard the cup shimmy and twist in the anonymous hand, mere yards away from where he now stood, and yet shrouded in veil upon veil of mystery...

Who could it *be*?

What did he know, and why did he know it?

What had Horus got himself into?

Finally, all sound on the other end came to a stop. The contact had surely wrangled the cup to his ear. Horus took his own cup away...

He replaced it in front of his snout...

"Omnibus Nantucket?"

Then, he listened...

He *waited*...

"Ten minutes. Farmer Nelson's Plaza. Get a seat at the trellis table. Be there, or be sorry."

Horus hadn't time to wonder at the voice – to his surprise, the voice of a woman – or the contents of its message, before he listened in on another whirl of action. The contact – the lady – was on the move!

Horus threw open his sliding door. He had no mind to kick the cloak and dagger overtures down the road another ten minutes. He'd get his answers now...

He rushed down the line of booths, even as his eyes darted ahead of him, homing for that magic number...

11... 12... 13...

He stopped cold. He looked frantically in all directions. But it was no use. The booths he could see only went up to 13...

Catching his breath, he cursed his luck. Then, he returned to the lobby...

The man at the counter jumped slightly as Horus clacked his hands on the board...

"Can you tell me where Farmer Nelson's Plaza is?"

* * *

"Here we are, Sir," the waitress gestured, showing Horus his table.

"Thank you, Miss," he replied, seating himself calmly, unobtrusively. "Lovely evening, isn't it?"

Her features drew back, just as if he'd said something crazy. "Well... I guess it's been uneventful so far... thankfully," she answered dubiously. "Do you know what you'd like to order, or should I give you a minute with the menu?"

"Nothing for me, thank you," Horus said, trying not to sound too eager to turn her down. He'd learned 'Farmer Nelson's' open-air restaurant was so named because its menu was strictly vegetarian. Even the attendant was hopeless to explain why, except to say that every place needs a gimmick. "I'm meeting a friend here," Horus went on to explain.

The waitress nodded. "Alright. Just let one of us know if you change your mind."

She withdrew with a nervous look about her. When she was gone, Horus dropped his polite smile, almost gagging...

Seated at the surprise second-checkpoint in this ongoing caper, he took in his surroundings afresh. He was practically the only soul in the entire little square of tables. The few people present appeared honest enough, if a little the worse for wear, as they hunched over their plates and poked at the contents. Horus could only sympathize. But he was glad to have such a clear line-of-sight. There were no walls out here... and he was seated essentially in the corner, just in front of a trellis at the end of a long hedge. He no longer lamented missing his chance to confront 'the lady' at the cup booth. She would have to meet him openly now...

"Meeting a *friend*, are we?" a deep, shadowy voice mocked him from behind. Horus' ears reflexively swiveled, even as the rest of him remained impassive. "That's a bit of a stretch, wouldn't you say?"

This left Horus feeling more than a little foolish. Naturally, the voice was coming through the dark weave of the trellis...

"It wouldn't seem your place to ask, whoever you are," Horus replied, eyes still trained forward. "I'm here to meet a contact from the Armada Inn. Would you presume to know something of our business?"

"Better check your own presumptions, *friend*," the voice answered. "How can you be sure the Inn contact and I aren't one and the same?"

"Simple. The one at the Inn was a woman."

There was a thoughtful silence.

"Very well," the voice said finally. "Rest assured that her part has been played. She sent you to *me*. I'm the one who has what you want."

"What exactly do you have?" Horus questioned. Whether consciously or by delayed reaction, his head began to swivel...

"Don't turn around!" the voice cautioned him. "You Mesomelae have keen eyes, and it's a bright night. You so much as flinch again and the deal's off. You get nothing. No time, no place..."

"I've already had more than my fill of both," he admitted boldly. "I came here for a name. Give me a *name*."

The voice settled into a menacing snicker. "You don't get to make the rules, friend. You take what I give you. Kapeesh?"

Horus could feel his jowls adhering to his teeth... but he relented. "I understand."

"Corner of 7th and Bridgewater. Two minutes. Don't be late."

With his attention drawn, Horus didn't even note the return of the waitress until it was too late. She surprised him...

"Excuse me, Sir, but someone sent you this pineapple sampler..."

Horus bolted up and around the edge of the trellis, nearly sending her tray flying. This second contact might've thought he could buy a discreet exit, but Horus didn't miss the sound of soles spinning out on the street, nor did he allow his otherwise superb manners to restrain him...

He made chase...

The mystery man had a healthy lead, paired with that impressive flight reflex that Humans were noted for. Horus had his determination. On the other hand, he also had a suit that was probably a size or two too small for a proper mad-dash. He'd meant to have the tailor let it out a bit anyway...

The no-goodnik made with all the simple tricks in the same tired order... ducking around a corner, throwing down a trash can behind him. Horus swerved and sprang as best he could, panting as he struggled not to lose a step...

What really started to wear him down was when they burst back into a main street, where foot traffic was dense. The common folk still shambling about with their eyes down, it was all Horus could do to push through without bowling them over. The fleeing villain, of course, had no such restraint, and a smaller frame to boot. Horus slowly watched the man fly on ahead, until he finally disappeared into the sea of other Humans. With naught to do but concede defeat, Horus jogged to a halt under a streetlamp, gasping for breath while his tongue dripped...

He paused and stewed only a few moments before resolving. He collected himself, recalling what the man had told him. There was still a trail to follow... a trail that might go just as cold as this fruitless chase, if he didn't act fast...

No sooner than Horus turned to go back the way he'd came, and he was brusquely knocked into by a passer-by. It was quite the collision... if the man had been nearly Horus' size, he probably would've been tackled...

"Have a care, would you?" he managed with a wave of his fist, biting back much stronger words. But the stranger paid no mind. And why should Horus be surprised? No one had been looking where they were going all night...

But before Horus might've continued on, he stopped, replaying the collision in his head. Suddenly, he was aware of himself... of his pockets. He checked them, feeling distinctly that he remembered a ruffle of paper in that moment of chaos...

And sure enough, in a breast pocket, he found a *note*...

Lt. Colonel Xavier Elitis. Grufthoffen Stalag.

Horus blinked, utterly dumbfounded. He looked up from the paper in his hand, eyes smartly settling on the answer to one mystery, at least. He read the street signs by the lamppost...

One read, '7th St.'

The other read, 'Bridgewater Blvd.'

He almost chuckled despite himself, returning his eyes to the note. Finally, it appeared he had a *name*. But what of the *place*? 'Grufthoffen

Stalag?' Was that where Tweed had left the body? Naturally, it didn't say. He checked both sides of the paper, but of course, there was no more.

Beginning to breathe a little easier, Horus withdrew from the open street, propping himself up against the post while he pondered. Obviously, he could draw no further conclusions from the note itself. But the night was still young. He was under enormous pressure to crack the Tweed case. And, more than anything, his own curiosity was piqued. There was no sense delaying another moment. He would ask around about the Stalag. He would learn all he could, *tonight*...

* * *

It didn't take long to get a line on Grufthoffen Stalag. Expecting by the name of it to be tucked away in some far-flung corner of Despotopia, Horus was quite surprised – and more than a little delighted – to learn the place had just gone up on the outskirts of St. Argonsburg proper. Within the span of two hours, he stood on its very threshold...

Intrepidly walking in, he flagged down the first officer he came across. "Excuse me, Sergeant," he called. "Excuse me. My name is Horus Templar – I'm a defense attorney working a potential murder case." He figured he'd lay it on heavy.

"*Murder*?" the Sergeant asked, sounding more unnerved than Horus would've expected from a military man. "You couldn't mean that Syzygy Killer case?!"

"I beg your pardon?" Horus replied. He had no prior familiarity with any 'Syzygy Killer' case. Perhaps he misheard...

"Well, never mind... I'm sure I don't want to know." He drew a Pi symbol in the air in front of him... possibly, he had a strong sailing background. "What can I do for you, Mr. Templar?"

"I need to inquire after a Lieutenant Colonel named Xavier Elitis. Has he recently come up missing?"

"Elitis? Missing?" The man succumbed to nervous laughter. "I certainly hope not! He's our senior prisoner!"

Horus' face bunched up. "Prisoner?"

The Sergeant nodded, all matter-of-fact. "That's right. This is a prisoner of war camp."

"Yes, I understand that," Horus replied. "Even so, if he were a prisoner, I would've expected quite a different name and rank. Oberstleutnant, perhaps..."

The army man's brow knit. But finally, something seemed to click. "Oh, no... we don't have any *Despotopian* prisoners here. That wouldn't make any sense!"

Horus was beside himself. "Wouldn't it? After all, didn't we just win a war with them?"

"Oh yes, we did!" the Sergeant went along happily. "But then... well..." he hesitated, stroking his chin in thought. "Heh, maybe I should just let ol' Col. Elitis explain it to you. I can show you to his barracks, if you like."

"Yes, please do," Horus nodded. Inwardly though, he was deeply puzzled... and not just because of this apparent misunderstanding as to the nature of the prison camp. No... one question presently drove out all others: What would he do *now*, if this Xavier Elitis actually turned out to be still alive? He shook his head, deploring to ask himself such a mercenary question...

* * *

The rather short but very secure road that followed had a way of taking Horus' hierarchy of questions and expertly reshuffling them. As Sgt. Pavlov led him into the prison yard, certain incongruencies began to surface. When Horus passed a surprise barracks inspection, it wasn't enough to double-take what he saw. He *stared*... feeling a visceral sense of displacement, as though he'd just been transported from a POW camp to army basic training. The officers conducting the roll call were all in a mix of Jast-Madiir service and combat uniforms. That much made perfect sense. But the ones playing the role of 'prisoners' – they were dressed in PT gear...

...*Jast-Madiiran* PT gear...

Horus couldn't make it add up. Pavlov had said there were no Despotopian inmates. That could've left Manean or Tophthaeran inmates, in theory... though it had been a long time since the last shooting war with either nation. But now, it appeared that *everyone* here was native. How could that be? He'd heard nothing of any mass desertions. Even if there had been, the deserters would only have been executed. What were droves of Jast-Madiiran POW's doing in a Jast-Madiiran prison camp?

He was shaken from his spiraling calculations as Pavlov reached and opened a barracks door...

"Col. Elitis!" he called into the small building... evidently a private officer's quarters. "A visitor to see you!"

Horus stepped up to the threshold, finding a solemn man seated with one arm on a rough-hewn little wooden table, facing the left wall. The man looked up and over at them slowly, shifting a toothpick in his mouth. His eyes managed to be sad and strong, while at the same time hinting at some quiet desperation. Horus wondered at him sitting there, wearing an off-duty jacket with his Lt.-Col. stripes pinned on. He was definitely Jast-Madiiran, and he was definitely a prisoner. On top of that, he was definitely *alive*...

"Who is this man, Pavlov?" Elitis asked in a gravelly tone, still sitting low on his bench. "I've never met him before."

"I'm Horus Templar," Horus answered on his own behalf. "I'm here to investigate a killing." He hesitated, trying to think what more he could say that still fit the facts. "It's been... *suggested* that you may have some connection with the case."

Here, Elitis made up his mind to stand, looking freshly surprised. "I think maybe I can help you after all. Come in, Mr. Templar – have a seat."

Horus nodded, choosing the adjacent bench. He joined Elitis sitting back down at the table, while Sgt. Pavlov left them to their business.

"So, a *killing*, you say?" Elitis began. "I've been expecting a sleuth to come calling for some time. But I guess I didn't realize how serious this really was."

"It *is* very serious... and rather urgent," Horus replied. "But if you were expecting a detective, you may be disappointed. Actually, I'm an attorney."

Elitis paused in nibbling his toothpick, eyes widening. "A lawyer? That's... rather remarkable. And far from disappointing. I won't deny... the idea of seeking legal counsel has been on my mind of late." He laughed. "Now, here you are, brought to me without so much as my asking."

Of course, Horus still had no idea what the man was talking about. But he reckoned there was time to get the answers he *really* came for... why not venture the other burning question first? "You'll understand, Mr. Elitis: I came here to get at the truth surrounding my client. I'm not sure there's anything I can do to help with *your* situation." Here came his operative segue. "In fact... I must confess I haven't the foggiest notion what sort of situation you're in."

The Lt. Colonel shrugged. "I'm just the man to tell you, if you're the least bit curious."

"Enlighten me."

Elitis forced a breath through his nose, taking his worn-down toothpick and chipping it into a cup filled with dozens just like it. "It's like this," he started. "And mind you, this is a tough yarn to follow."

"I guessed as much. Go ahead."

"Well, I was in the war... the war we just won against Despotopia. Only, I didn't fare as well as most. My group was captured shortly after we made landfall by a whole battalion of Despotopian soldiers."

Horus noted Elitis pause. "I'm sure I follow you so far," he encouraged him.

"Right. Anyway, they shipped us off to one of their Stalags. It was a few weeks of open-pit mining and scratching by on kidney beans. That was about the time the High Constable turned the tables."

"Yes," Horus remarked. "Of all our victories against Despotopia, the latest is surely among the most extraordinary."

"You can imagine my surprise," Elitis nodded. "Here we are – imprisoned – and suddenly we're told the war is over, practically just when it was getting started. Despotopia is forced to admit defeat... their own beloved Kaiser is taken hostage! It felt personal. It felt like *retribution*. At least, at first it did..."

"What happened next?"

"Well, we *waited*," Elitis explained. "We had every reason to expect our rescue was coming. Either we'd be rounded up after the reparations were negotiated, or possibly even as part of Despotopia's ransom for Hienrechenshlagen. The first few weeks still in camp were hopeful. The next few grew uneasy. But within a month, we were sure we'd been forgotten."

"The generals never bargained for your release?"

"Clearly, they didn't." Elitis gestured around them. "Here I am."

"So I see," Horus went along. "But of course, *that's* what I still fail to understand."

"I'll explain it to you the way the Constable's men explained it to me. Running a prison camp is, well, an *expense*... in money, manpower, and consumables. A poor country like Despotopia evidently couldn't spare one or more of those indefinitely. But they couldn't very well just *let* us go, either... their defeat was humiliation enough. So, how to keep us, their hard-won prisoners of war?"

"I'm sure I don't know."

"Simple. They *outsourced* us."

Horus looked on blankly only for a moment. Then it hit him. His eyes danced across the table as he worked to make sure all the pieces fit the way he supposed. "You mean...?" he began, hard-pressed to even put it into words. "You're saying they...?"

"That's right," Elitis confirmed. "The Despotopians hired out to have someone else keep us prisoner *for* them."

"And... *Jast-Madiir* made an offer?"

"*The* offer." He turned up his hands. "After all, they stood to make some money off it. So now, my men and I are being kept in a Jast-Madiir-run Despotopian prison camp for Jast-Madiiran soldiers."

Horus searched for words befitting his sympathy and disbelief. "That's... that's rather strange. And inconvenient, I'm sure."

"You can't imagine," Elitis sighed, plopping back on his bench, turning down a shell-shocked look. "I don't even know what to do with myself, Mr. Templar. As the senior ranking POW officer, I'm duty-bound to attempt escape. If I never get out – or even *try* – it's capital dereliction of duty. But on the other hand, if I *do* escape, my own countrymen will only hunt me down as a fugitive. I can't win."

Horus shook his head. "I can see why you might've been interested in legal counsel."

The desperate look in Elitis' eyes finally broke loose. "Mr. Templar, *can* you help me? I'm not sure how long I can keep it together in here. All I want is to go back to serving my country the old-fashioned way."

"I'll see what I can do for you," Horus assured him. "As I understand it, the High Constable is still working out Despotopia's payment plan for the extradition of Kaiser Hienrechenshlagen. And, as luck would have it, I'm also told that he'll be inspecting the SAPD in the coming days. Perhaps I can arrange a meeting with him – see if I can convince him to make a prisoner exchange part of the bargain."

Col. Elitis grinned, inclining his head. "I'd thank you to do that."

"Gladly," Horus replied, before waxing grave. "But then, I still need to know what you can do for *me*." He leaned in with a searching gaze. "Tell me, Mr. Elitis: What does the name Arcadian Tweed mean to you?"

Elitis' already distressed eyes managed to bulge even further for just a moment before he averted them. He grabbed up a fresh toothpick to mangle. "I'll certainly tell you... for what it's worth," he said. "He spent some time under my command, back when I was in charge of a platoon in the Foreign Legion."

Horus blanched. "Tweed... was in the *military*?"

Elitis nodded. "It was only for a little while; he never even deployed. But it's no trouble remembering the name. Even among volunteer soldiers from other countries, he was a bit unconventional. Said he joined up because he liked the hats."

"That's definitely our Tweed," Horus quipped. "But what about his crime? What's your connection with that?"

Elitis took the toothpick from his mouth, twisting it into the board until its end rolled back. "*His* crime? I'm... not sure I follow."

Horus was becoming alarmed. He'd formed all this rapport, and now, for no reason he could imagine, his one good lead seemed to be clamming up. "But you *said* you were expecting a sleuth," Horus reminded him, hoping to trap him in his own words. "What for, if not to tell me who it is that Tweed killed?"

"Tweed... *killed*?" Elitis' face contorted. "Mr. Templar, I think there's been some awful mistake..."

"*No* mistake," Horus pressed him. "Mr. Elitis, I've had a long, difficult night. I've been led by the scruff of my neck all over the city, chasing phantoms... just to get the *name* of Tweed's victim. Don't withhold it from me now."

"But I don't have it!" Elitis lamented. "I'm no part of this. Not *really*. What little I know came down the pipe anonymously. I was told to give a name alright... but not the name of any *victim*. I was only supposed to give you the name of the man that could tell you who the victim is!"

Horus sank in his seat. He let out a belabored sigh. "*Of course*. One more link in the chain." He set an elbow on the table, propping up his head in his hand. "Alright, Elitis. Let's have it."

There was no immediate response. "I'll give you the name I was given," Elitis said, low and reserved. "...But you're not going to like it."

"No doubt," Horus quipped. "Go ahead, just the same."

Elitis grimaced. He coaxed his lips just to form the words...

...And then, he spoke *the name*...

Chapter 7

"You!" Horus called, marching aggressively on the cell, just as if the bars couldn't hold him back. "You must think you're incredibly clever, sending me far and wide on that wild goose chase!"

Tweed didn't even bother to put down the newspaper. "What seems to be the problem, Mr. Templar?" he asked. "Are you here to chew me out because you failed the mission?"

"Worse!" Horus replied. "I'm here because I *succeeded*. I found your old commanding officer, alright. I found Xavier Elitis. He said he'd give me the name of the man who could identify your victim. He then proceeded to give me *your* name!"

"Of course," Tweed said, folding the paper in his lap. "Who would know better than me?"

Horus' jowls fluttered, wanting to showcase the fangs behind them, though he restrained himself. "But *why*, then?!" he demanded. "Why send me through this whole elaborate smoke-and-mirrors routine, if in the end I was only going to be sent back to *you*?"

Tweed shrugged widely. "It seemed like the only thing I could do to make you people understand just how deep into this thing I really am."

Horus sighed, massaging the space between his eyes. "Well, alright. You've made your point. You certainly led me straight to the innermost circle of this whole conspiracy. I played your game; I jumped through your hoops. I hope you're appeased." He looked up. "Now, will you humor me, and let me finish what I started? Will you name your victim, so we can all move forward?"

The crazy little man shook his head. "Sorry, Mr. Templar. That just doesn't seem like something the Syzygy Killer would do."

"The Syzygy Killer?" Horus repeated, recalling the strange reference from earlier that night. "Whatever do you mean?"

"What? You haven't heard about my alter ego?"

"I've heard the term mentioned once before... just hours ago, when I was at the Stalag. I'd like to know where on earth it came from."

Tweed whipped his newspaper at the bars. "Honestly, I don't know where you've been all day... even if I sent you there myself. I'm on my third headline already! Late breaking news – a special edition..."

Horus reached in and took up the paper. He opened it and read the feature story. The *only* story...

"'Syzygy Killer – A **Cannibal**?'" He blanched. "This... this is about you?"

"It surprised me, too," Tweed admitted. "It's exciting, in a way – I'm learning new things about myself all the time! But I have to admit, eating people feels like more than I bargained for." He stroked his chin in puzzlement. "Do you think it would still count if I only eat hair and nail clippings?"

"Tweed..." Horus started over, mustering what delicacy he could. Outrage wasn't getting him anywhere. He'd have to try other angles of attack. "I must urge you not to get caught up in this... this fallacious bit of reporting." Horus certainly *hoped* it was fallacious. "Don't let this persona the newspeople are building around you dictate your actions. Don't worry about what a 'Syzygy Killer' would do." Yes, maybe Horus had something here. He'd learned tonight that Tweed had been in the Foreign Legion for a time. What else might he discover? What could he learn about the man that might inform the investigation? Maybe this was a good opportunity to find out... "You must ask yourself: What would *Arcadian Tweed* do? What are *his* principles? What is his outlook on the world? Who has he always meant to be? Surely, there is a piece of you which has aspired to some virtue..."

Tweed thought about this deeply. "Well, I remember growing up, I always wanted to be an old miser," he recalled at length. "You know? The kind that pinches every penny – that burns every bridge in his life and generally deals with people ruthlessly, year after long year..."

Horus blinked. "*That's* the part of you that aspired to be virtuous?"

Tweed nodded. "Right. Because, the thing is, everyone loves an old miser in the end! Like, lifelong-generous people are so boring – the nice things they do are just tedious after a while. But if you're an *old miser*, and you're nice to people *just one time*, then suddenly you're everybody's favorite person in the whole world! That's what I wanted to be. I wanted to live out a whole life of greedy snobbery, just so I could surprise everyone with sudden, unsolicited charity and be a folk hero forever!" He shrugged. "Too bad I was never any good with my finances."

Horus mused, curling his whiskers. "I have to admit, I can actually see a bit of distorted merit to that whole idea." He grinned, perhaps too mischievously. "More than that, I think I see a way for you to live out your dream... in a manner of speaking."

Tweed looked on with an expectant sort of confusion. "You do?"

"I do." Horus began to pace before the bars, arms folded behind him. "Consider this, Arcadian: As we speak, there's an entire police department up in arms, turning the city inside-out, trying to obtain that which is in your power to give them." He waved the paper at him. "More than that, you've evidently captured the imagination of the entire population. Without even meaning to, perhaps, you've created this menacing identity for yourself... and St. Argonsburg is greatly disquieted. Why not do that *one generous thing*, and end your own reign of terror? Tell us who you killed. Make a clean breast of the whole thing. Let the truth have its day, so that we can dispel all this mystery and superstition that's suddenly gripped the country. Believe me, I couldn't imagine a more charitable act on your part if I tried."

"Hmm..." Tweed contemplated. "It has a certain logic to it..."

Horus tried not to make a face, hearing Tweed assess his powers of logic. But he waited expectantly for the verdict...

"Sorry, Mr. Templar," Tweed said at last. "I'm afraid Arcadian Tweed has no more taste for logic than the Syzygy Killer does."

Horus glared. He'd had his fill of this insanity, and to spare. He wanted nothing more right now than to enlist the help of the guards, bind Tweed with his eyes held open and *look* into them until he was absolutely forced to reveal the identity of the man he killed... and many sad, stupid little secrets besides. And after all, wouldn't it be the right thing to do? Yes... clearly he'd been too soft before. Tweed's reticence was causing exceptional grief not only for his friends and colleagues, but now, apparently, the entire city! What right did one man have to hold a *city* hostage?

It was in Horus' power to stop this, here and now. He *could* do it. He *should* do it. Besides, he'd already forced the truth out of Tweed once before...

But then, his ears folded back – his gaze fell. Yes, he'd forced Tweed into a prior confession. But that was *before* he was his client...

"You know, the police will only keep trying," Horus said in a low voice, for what it was worth. "You know you're only delaying the inevitable."

"More *reasons*," Tweed retorted. "Don't you see? It's no use." He smiled again, and it turned Horus' stomach. "Besides, they're never gonna figure it out. Not *ever*."

Before Horus could invent some scalding rebuttal, a voice flanked him from the side...

"There you are." It was the Deputy Constable, approaching with Captain Alexei, Ms. Cordon, and even Art and Deborah all in step. "They said you'd returned. Naturally, I expected you to report straight to Blackforest. Instead we find you here." He spied the paper in Horus' hand, pointing it out. "Catching up on current events, are we? Or, do we have *you* to thank for this... *outlandish* story? Were you ever going to bring us up to speed on what you've learned, Templar? Or were we just supposed to read about it in black and white?"

Horus shook his head. "You've got this all wrong, Milo. Blackforest's office was my next stop. If I was in no hurry to see him, it's only because my errand proved as fruitless as I feared. There's nothing new to tell." He unrolled the paper in front of him. "As for the story... I honestly hoped *you* could shed some light on that. Don't you have any notion where they got the idea that Tweed was... well, a *cannibal*?"

"Well I'm quite sure *I* don't know," Miloje spouted gruffly. "Who can say where they dig up these whimsical farces? I honestly wouldn't put it past those nefarious newsmen to invent such nonsense on the spot, if for a moment I could believe they have the real estate for powers of imagination somewhere in their tiny, twisted minds."

At once, both Art and Alexei cleared their throats, and proceeded to scan the hall nonchalantly. Art even began to whistle. Miloje turned a grimace on both of them in turn...

"Well?" he demanded. "I should like to know what the two of you are suddenly so inconspicuous about. Don't think I didn't hear your little grunts. I'm elderly, but not deaf. What do you have to say for yourselves?"

"Only that I'm with you, Chiefy," Art said. "I can't imagine where the whole cannibal idea came from. Certainly not from me – I can tell ya that much. Yes, sir."

Miloje eyed Art suspiciously for a moment. But then, he turned his look on Alexei. "How about you, *Captain*? Any worthwhile tidbits?"

"Dear me, *no*," Alexei snickered nervously. "I only meant to say... or, well... I do find myself wondering if..." He kneaded his thin fingers until they were an unidentifiable knot. "Well, there are times – recent ones – where I think that perhaps we've developed a somewhat lower opinion of reporters than they truly merit. After all, are we really quite certain they're as loathsome as we make them out? Surely, they cannot be all *that* bad."

Miloje raised an eyebrow. "You're one for pushing your luck, aren't you? Those physical stunts you used to pull were one thing... I wonder if you guess how close you are to *real* disaster, spouting such heresies in my presence! I have plenty of time now to train up Captain Brocksmith as my replacement instead of you, you know."

"Don't let that nasty little kid push you around like that!" Tweed unexpectedly put in. "You're a tall fella, and he's just a shrimp. You can take him!"

"I beg your pardon!" Miloje huffed, turning another accusatory look into Tweed's cell. "Did I really just hear you refer to me as a *child*?!"

"You sure did, *Tinker Tot*!" Tweed riposted, taking hold of his bars. "Why don't you go crying to your mommy about it?"

"Well of all the...!" Miloje stammered. "I don't need to stand here and accept such slander! It should be exceptionally plain – even to *you* – my youth is well-buried in the folds of time. I'm a very old man!"

"Whatever you need to tell yourself, Sprout," Tweed persisted. "Take away all that age, and what've you got left? Nothing but a little *brat*!"

"Come away from it, Miloje – you know it's no use," Blucille urged him. "We should take this thing where the peanut gallery won't bother us."

"Indeed," Miloje sighed his agreement. "Things *are* a little too nutty here for my taste." He turned a last fiery glance back at Tweed, an amused grin accentuating his many wrinkles. "But this isn't over," he boded.

"Any time you think you're man enough, Shorty. I'm not scared of *you*!"

Miloje shrugged. "I've been counted out before. But I've made a habit of shocking my critics, in the end." He tipped his police bobby and stepped away, following the rest...

"So is it true?" Miloje asked Horus, who'd lingered behind, waiting up for him. "Are we really on the way to Blackforest's office, only to report nothing at all?"

"It's true," Horus admitted. "It's not a fact I'm looking forward to sharing. Hamilton clearly hasn't been of the best disposition lately."

"He's not the only one mad enough to dice furniture with his bare hands right now," Miloje grumbled. "I say let him put on his dramatic tantrums if it suits him. But don't you soon forget: A visit by the High Constable is not my cup of tea, either. In fact, between Blackforest and myself, I would say I get the worse part. If I manage a bit more decorum than he does, it is only a credit to my longsuffering."

"Maybe not as much decorum as you think," Horus suggested quietly, trying to inject some discretion into their conversation. They were far enough behind the rest of the group that they could go unheard, if they kept things low. "I can take you jumping on *my* back now and again, Milo... by now, I *expect* it. But I don't think you needed to go off on Alexei the way you did."

Miloje sighed. "You haven't had to work with him lately. He's been an insufferable fidgety wreck ever since his return from the marriage office."

Horus eyed him. "Marriage?"

"You'll recall his abrupt departure yesterday. Turns out he *was* on State business. He'd been conscripted and summoned to his wedding."

"*Incredible*," Horus breathed. "I mean, it would have to be quite a big change for him, suddenly having a wife. I'm... sure it takes some adjusting to."

"Well, he'd better not dally about adjusting. Most of us have to, sooner or later."

"I do wonder at times why you're always so impatient with him."

"Shouldn't I be? He *is* to replace me."

"That's another thing I've never truly understood," Horus ventured, scratching his chin. "Why *him*, Milo?" He held up defensive hands. "I mean no disrespect. I'm only curious: How does the self-proclaimed bumpkin from Podunkville wind-up the prime candidate for Deputy Constable?"

"For the same reason he was upgraded to the SAPD in the first place," Miloje explained. "His outstanding achievements can't be wholly excused, though I might try."

"What achievements? For all his folksy recounts of Podunkville, I can't recall that he's ever mentioned anything pertaining to his career."

"I'm sure his modesty prevents him, which is only another of his frustrating idiosyncrasies," Miloje muttered. "Besides that, I think it remains somewhat a sore spot for him. Long story short, he broke up a major blackmail ring that was infesting his small town, and a few surrounding settlements besides." The Deputy Constable skipped a beat. "It is rather a sad story, actually. But as much as I hate to admit it, his is also among the finest tales of police work in our day and age."

This came as no small surprise. "I'm... I'm rather amazed. I wouldn't have guessed there was so much to our Captain Alexei all along."

"Yes, I am sure it's hard to accept. But somewhere in that stringy, awkward frame of his is the mind and heart of an exemplary officer."

They slowed up even more, dropping their line of conversation when they suddenly noticed the rest of the group had come to a halt ahead of them...

"Well, I'd say we're out of earshot," Blucille explained. "Before we go any further, I'd like a few words with Templar. *Alone*, if possible."

"Just as well," Miloje replied. "I'm satisfied he's gotten no place."

"I'm gonna buzz off, too," Art put in. "Debby and I have some catching up to do."

Blucille suddenly looked quite surprised, and perhaps a little hurt. "But I thought you and I were still on for dinner?"

"Oh, we are, no problem!" he assured her. "I'm not *leaving*-leaving – just stepping away for a minute. Like I said, I have some stuff to talk about with Deborah." He waved his hands in the air. "Nothing unusual or even interesting, mind you. Like, just friendly small-talk. Shootin' the breeze. Chattin' about the weather and boring stuff like that. Ya know?"

Deborah clapped her hand against her head.

"*...Oh-kay...*" Blucille replied. "Well, just remember: I'm taking my dinner break at 0:30. See you then?"

"Wouldn't dream of missing it," Art winked. He waved his goodbyes to all gathered. "See ya Counselor, Captain, Deputy Constable, Pooky Face."

Horus watched as Deborah began to depart with him, unable to help a look of incomprehension. Deborah only shrugged apologetically and turned to go.

"What was that about?" Blucille asked Horus in a quiet voice.

"I don't know," he admitted. "It was a little strange, wasn't it?"

"I wonder how you can tell strange from normal, with one such as Mallard," Miloje quipped.

"It wasn't so much what *he* said," Horus explained. "That Deborah went along is what puzzles me."

"Well, don't ponder it overlong. We still have a real case to solve." The Deputy Constable turned to his understudy. "Come along, Alexei."

"Yes, Sir."

Horus watched the Captain leave, seeing him in a new light. Apparently, he was a man of quiet brilliance. And – presently – of quiet *disquiet*... if the drawn-back way his face was frozen provided any clue. Horus could only infer that something about Alexei's new wife had him frazzled, though he couldn't hope to guess what. All he could say for sure was that Miloje would be no help. Horus would have to see about speaking with Alexei himself at some point...

...For now, it was time to return to business...

"Well, here we are," Horus said, turning to Blucille. "You already know *my* mission was a botch. How is yours going?"

"I have a few of our investigators supervising a team of Berlberi Clerks," she explained. "We'll have all the Embassy's records audited very soon. And – last I knew – the Boss suspects nothing." Horus was quite pleased to hear it. Everything she *said* was very promising. Even so, her features didn't read very confident...

"But...?"

She groaned. "But nothing, I guess. I just can't fight the feeling that I've stuck my neck out a little too far on this one."

"It'll be fine. We only stand to benefit from anything we learn." He chuckled. "What could we possibly discover that would make things *worse*?"

"I suppose you're right," she nodded evasively. "But getting Blackforest to see it that way is still another matter altogether."

"Don't worry," he encouraged her. Then he started on his way again. "When I get through talking with Hamilton, I don't think he'll have any rage left to vent on you."

* * *

"That was real smooth, Art," Deborah grumbled. "While you were at it, you should've added, *'It's not like we're gonna talk about how she's turning into a Werehuman, or anything'*."

"I don't sound like that," he rebutted. "And anyway, that would've been a stupid thing to say."

She sighed, rubbing the back of her neck. "Never mind. What did you find out?"

"Nothing but good news. You're in the clear, Debs. The shoes smelled all wrong. On toppa that, the zoo's got four or five animals they can't account for."

"*Thank the Creators*," she breathed as her shoulders dropped. But quickly, she looked unsure... unsatisfied. "You're 100% certain, though? I mean, there's absolutely no chance I ate this guy?"

He finger-gunned her with an apologetic grin. "Let me smell your breath?"

She made a face at him. But then, she huffed at his snout while he took a deep *WHIFF*...

"Nope!" he confirmed. "You're good!"

"Well, I'm *glad* of that."

"Me too," Art nodded emphatically. "It's always so nice when a case is open and shut like this." He clapped his hands together. "Now, if you'll excuse me, I have a dinner date..."

"Wait!" she called after him. "You can't just call off the investigation *now*!"

"I *can't*? Why not?" he asked, genuinely perplexed. "You wanted to know if you ate somebody, and you didn't. How could we be any more finished here?"

She shook her head. "We still haven't got at the root of the problem. We still don't know if I might be a danger to society... anytime I *transform*..."

He groaned. "Well, okay then! If you're gonna be that way about it, we still don't even know for sure if you *do* transform!"

"Oh, not this again!" She threw up her hands. "I thought I made you understand this thing is for *real*, Art. Remember that my great-grandfather used to change around these alignments..."

"Uh-huh. And what did you ever see to prove it? Just a bolted cellar."

She turned away, running her hands over her folded ears. "*Okay*. I guess there's only one way to be sure. Heck knows I could use the sleep..." She looked back at him. "I need you to watch my house."

Art's brows drew in. "What, like... now? *Tonight*?"

"Is there some reason you can't?"

"I'm having *dinner* tonight," he reminded her. "How about tomorrow?"

"Okay then, tomorrow."

He shook his head. "Nah, tomorrow's no good, either."

She rolled her eyes. "Why not?"

"I'm having dinner then, too."

"UGH!" She curled tight little fists. "Look, Art: You and Blucille dating is honestly really sweet. I admit I didn't think it could work at first, but I see it's been good for you both. But for the love of *Pete*, can't you cancel on her *just one night*?! This is important!"

He leaned against the wall, striking a thoughtful pose. He pondered a spell. Then, he snapped. "Maybe the answer was at the zoo all along!"

"What do you mean?"

"Well, suppose I got an expert to swear there's no such thing as Werehumans. Would that ease your mind? Would that convince you that this is all just in your head?"

She looked at him utterly bewildered. "An expert? An expert on *what*?"

"Everything!" he explained. "I just need to find that world-famous Thinker... what was his name? Goldbloom!"

"Bronzegloom," she corrected him.

"Right, that guy. He's about the most famous Thinker there is... I think. If anybody would know for sure whether Werehumans are real or not, I'm sure it's him!"

"Well there's just one problem with that," Deborah boded. "You'd have to go all the way to the Wading Isle to talk to Bronzegloom. That's where he lives."

"For *real*?" he whined. "*Gagh*, what a pain in the neck..."

"Still, he's not the only Thinker out there..." she mused. "I'm sure there's at least one living here in St. Argonsburg. There almost has to be."

"If there is, I'll find out," he resolved. "And, if it turns out that Werehumans are just a buncha claptrap, *then* can I have my date tomorrow?"

Deborah deliberated on this point for a while.

"I won't say *yes*..." she answered finally. "But maybe."

"Works for me!" he smiled. "Thanks, Debs."

* * *

Horus found himself inert just outside Hamilton's door. Standing there, almost close enough to get a splinter in his nose, he wasn't sure why he even hesitated. Of course, it was one thing to report that Tweed had duped him... that would certainly be disappointing. But on top of that, he had his word to Col. Elitis to keep: He would have to seek Hamilton's help setting up a little chat with the High Constable... and he would have to do it without any barter. Considering Hamilton's mood over the whole inspection, Horus could safely infer that the last thing he wanted to deal with was trying to work-in any modifications to the Constable's itinerary...

...Not that Horus was at all afraid to set off Hamilton. No, as he stood there mustering resolve to go in, he knew it was merely his respect for the DA that made him loath to ruin his day all over again. That, and a general wish to avoid seeing the way that Hamilton had 'rearranged' his office. For them to talk business amid sheer entropy, having to pretend it was still a functional workspace, seemed a bit of a faux pas...

But finally, Horus knocked.

"Come in," he heard.

Horus opened the door slowly – surprised and relieved to find the room much as he'd last saw it... with only a few obvious but tasteful substitutions. Blackforest stood from his desk...

"Good evening, Horus." He gestured at a brand-new chair. "I don't suppose I can interest you in a seat? That isn't generally your way, when you're here to share bad news."

Horus blinked. "You already know the news is bad?"

"I can't see why else you'd linger outside my door that way," he explained. "So, you let Tweed lead you around the bend, eh?"

"*Four* bends, making a closed circuit. All along, he was pointing me to the one man who would have complete knowledge of his crime. Which was, of course, himself."

Blackforest chuckled. "That's almost funny. Maybe more than almost."

"Even so, my loss is your loss," Horus said, a bit surprised with himself. He came in expecting to tread on eggshells – now suddenly, he was more or less trying to drag Hamilton down with him. But after all, he was still pretty put-out himself about the whole misadventure...

"Strange to hear that coming from you, of all people," Hamilton quipped. "But I *am* glad you've been on our side in this. The last thing we needed was to assign Tweed an attorney who would only help him suppress evidence."

"I still firmly believe that's the last thing *he* needs, as well," Horus nodded. "I'll be honest, Hamilton – I don't believe Tweed has the slightest remorse for what he did. But even to *act* as if he had any remorse at all would be some small redemption. His cooperation with the authorities holds the key. But I can't get him to see that. I'm no more likely to solve this mystery than anyone." Arriving at this conclusion, Horus paused, remembering his *power* – the *look* he'd been so conflicted about employing of late. He set his muzzle into his curled fingers, deliberating whether to confide such things in Hamilton. Likely, the DA would only encourage his use of *the look* to bring the Tweed case to its rightful conclusion. But then, Blackforest also possessed a measure of this ability. Horus had seen him use it more than once... even at surprising range, in some instances. Who would better understand the terrible responsibility that came with it?

"...Then again, perhaps I *am*," he quietly ventured.

Blackforest's ears snapped fully forward. "What do you mean?"

"You know... *that look*... Hamilton?" he asked outright. "The one that compels people to tell the truth, even despite themselves?"

"Well of course I do," Blackforest admitted. "Who better? But I don't see wha..."

"...I used it on *Tweed*, Hamilton," Horus rushed his confession. "That's what started this whole mess. He was hinting around at something awful he did on the stand, and I gave him *the look*. That's the only reason we know he killed a man. I used *the look* on a whim, and what's come of it? I unwittingly plunged the SAPD into a fiasco. But now, I can't help wondering if it's the only way back out..."

There was a beat of apparently solemn, thoughtful silence. But then, Blackforest laughed out loud. "Now that's rich, Horus! I've seen your *look*. It's not even that good!"

Horus frowned. He looked away. And then, to prove his point, he *looked* back...

Blackforest's laughter ended abruptly as his eyes widened. "Okay, so it's not that *bad*, either," he admitted.

Horus' gaze sunk. "I've had this ability for a long time... but now, when we need it most, I suddenly find myself with questions of conscience I've never faced before. Does it betray my duty as a Public Defender to use it on my own client? After all: All I'm trying to get at is the truth. And the truth is *always* right, no matter how inconvenient. So what's stopping me? Why can't I follow through on this?"

"I think you've already answered that, Counselor," Hamilton said, and Horus was surprised at the sympathetic quality of his voice. "You want Tweed to cooperate – to show some remorse. If you drag the truth out of him kicking and screaming, you deny him that chance forever. Deep down, you knew that... even if you couldn't put it into words."

Horus looked back up, feeling much unexpected admiration and gratitude. "Well thank you, Hamilton. You know, you make it easy to forget what a good man you are sometimes."

Blackforest smiled deviously. "Maybe not as good as you think. Personally, Horus, I think your inner struggle is for naught. Remember that as the prosecutor in this case, I don't share your obligation to Tweed. I already tried to *look* the truth out of him. It didn't work. Yours wouldn't, either." He shrugged. "Some people are just too strong-willed."

"But that doesn't fit," Horus argued. "Like I said, he only confessed his killing in the first place because I *looked* at him." Now it was Horus who smiled deviously. "I think maybe you're avoiding the obvious conclusion: My *look* is simply better than yours."

Blackforest huffed. "Keep dreaming. And why don't you show yourself out, while you're at it? You've obviously still got your work cut out for you." His eyes rolled to the ground. "And I'm in for a *big day* tomorrow..." he forced through his fangs.

A nervous chuckle escaped before Horus could choke it back. "Yes, your big day..." he began, seeing he'd been handed his operative segue. "I don't suppose you might prevail upon the High Constable to have a quick word with a lowly public servant, such as myself?"

To say that Blackforest appeared unimpressed with this new line of questioning was a gross understatement. "What about?" he asked. It was not a friendly-sounding question.

"It's a rather complicated matter," Horus explained at his own fingers. "I don't suppose you're familiar with a one Grufthoffen Stalag?"

"I've heard of it..." Blackforest admitted.

"Well, what do you think of it?"

"I think what the High Constable does with the *military* is none of my business," he answered as he folded his arms. "And certainly none of yours. What's your sudden interest?"

"I met with a Lieutenant Colonel there tonight, as part of Tweed's little rat-race. I promised him I would at least attempt to make his release a part of the Kaiser's extradition bargain."

Blackforest ran a hand over his head. "Of *course* you would do something like that."

Horus shrugged apologetically. "Sorry, Hamilton. You know how I feel about injustice."

"Oh, I know. You just can't help yourself, can you?"

The room locked itself into a quiet stalemate. Blackforest worked his jaw back and forth, while Horus waited...

"Well?" he ventured at length.

Blackforest groaned. "Fine. I'll arrange your talk." He forced a small laugh. "If nothing else, it'll be a welcome reversal to watch someone try to back the *Constable* into a corner during one of these inspections." But then, he shot Horus a warning with his eyes. "Just see that you don't dig us any deeper into this hole you've stumbled on, Horus. Your streak of unearthing things better left buried is starting to stack up. I don't want any more trouble because of it. Are we clear on that?"

Remembering the secret investigation he'd already set Ms. Cordon on, Horus suddenly found himself sharing in her sincere hope that Blackforest wouldn't find out. He tugged at his collar with a toothy grin on his face.

"Yes. Quite clear."

Chapter 8

Art could hardly believe his good fortune. As the new day dawned, he soon discovered that not only was there a *Thinker* living in St. Argonsburg, but what sounded better still: a *Loremaster*. The information desk was kind enough to provide both name and street-address. And so, Art was bound for 1576 Braintrust Bluff, there to meet none other than the famed academic heavyweight known as Silbadilio. Art could be quite sure he was famous, because he vaguely recalled hearing his name a time or two before – which, for as much as he paid attention to the admittedly fashionable but extremely boring world of the intelligentsia, had to account for something.

Quiet, happy tunes passed Art's jowls as he strolled into a gated community. Such was his relief at finding a respected know-it-all who could lay the question of Werehumans to rest – in plenty of time for his date tonight – he almost managed not to notice the way the Other Worlds were once again pointing out his path from above. Honestly – if only in the back of his mind – it began to seem that they were *always* doing that. Like, even when he turned a corner or two...

Fortunately, before he could really start to think about it, Art reached his destination: a swanky, pillary house with a marble stoop. At the top of the steps, he craned his nose down to the sign on the door:

Residence of Thinker and Loremaster Silbadilio, PhDs

Consultation by Appointment Only, Excepting Walk-Ins

Art made only token effort to decipher this before resolving to simply knock...

He reached out...

KNOCK-KNOCK-KN...

To his surprise, his rolled-up fingers were left hanging in space only two-fifths of the way through his third knock. And there, immediately behind the open door, was a Meduseldan – sleek and swank in something of a custom-tailored black turtleneck with a collar wide enough to leave the blue, glowy top of his headless body uncovered. Completing the ensemble – balancing on the curled-up ends of his two right-most tentacles – was a pair of exquisitely carved bubble-pipes.

Never mind how strange it was to meet the master of the house at the front door, less than a second after he commenced rapping on it. Art knew at once: there was no mistaking the man by his duds. Surely, he could only be...

"...Silbadilio?"

"*Silbadilio*?" 'Silbadilio' repeated, unsure. "Is *that* all you have come to ask of me? But please, there *must* be more!"

Art looked on – still a bit flabbergasted – finding this response to be somewhat of an impasse. "Depends. I mean, you *are* Silbadilio, aren't you?"

"Am *I* Silbadilio?" the Meduseldan replied, throwing the question back at Art again. "My boy, I am Chair of the Cabinet of Albalast, Headmaster of Erudition Community College, Keeper of the Secret Frying Pan, standard-bearer in the Order of the Shallot, three-time recipient of the International Cranium Unobtanium Prize, mortarboard magnate and cosmopolitan cosmologist extraordinaire!"

"*Wow*," Art breathed. "You're really all that stuff?"

"*Brh*-Ha!" he laughed. "No more than half of it, as a rule. But as to your original question, you may indeed refer to me as Silbadilio... if only because that is my name."

Art took a moment to study Silbadilio, then. He'd only learned earlier this morning that there was any such thing as 'Loremasters,' and already his presumptions about them seemed to be right on the money...

"Okay," he replied.

"...Well, now we have one matter laid to rest," Silbadilio segued. "Surely there is something else I can assist you with! You certainly appear to have a parcel of unclaimed real-estate upstairs; who better than me to help you clutter it all up? You would surely be amazed at the abundance of information I possess, both factual and otherwise. It is yours to share in! What do you seek?"

"Well, I was hoping you could..." Art began, even as Silbadilio waved him into his house. But he hit a mental snag, as his mind played back through the drivel so far... "...Hang on a minute... did you say, 'factual and otherwise'? Like, what kind of 'otherwise' are we talkin' here?"

"Foolscap!" Silbadilio answered joyfully. "Rubbish, hogwash, fiddle-faddle. Sheer nonsense, of course!"

"But... why would you offer to tell me nonsense? Wouldn't that kinda go against what it means to be a 'Loremaster'?"

"*Blrhem*! Certainly not! Quite the contrary, in fact... my scholarly side alone would never suffice to make an honest Loremaster of me. The equal part of my toil must always be to supplement knowledge with empty hooey."

Art shook his head. "I don't get it. You're saying part of your *job* is to make up junk?"

"To a very high professional standard, yes. Does that indeed surprise you? Where it should not, my boy! For mine is the Dominion which is known for peddling in whimsical nonsense – the Prosketosa Daffadars! Are you perchance also ignorant of this? Of the way that each Dominion of the Meduselda has found some niche over the Eras, into which it has largely finessed itself? Fear not! There is a teaching song that relates this point well enough..."

He reached for a small pouch under his sweater, bringing up a tuning fork and a tiny mallet. He struck, and quickly thereafter made a sound like clearing his throat. Somehow, even in this strictly preparatory phase, Art could sense the forthcoming tone-deafness on a visceral level...

"Give ear y***e*** simpletons as I reh***ea***rse

Ten leg***a***cies for ten D***o***minions in verse:

The T***a***ltaxik***ho***..."

"*Okay!...* okay," Art exclaimed, waving the Loremaster down. "I think I'll do alright without all that. No offense, but a Sowür Canpattel you are not."

"*Brh*-Ah, well-said! I see you know something of what I would expound after all."

"Enough to get by. What I still don't understand is: How can making stuff up be part of your job as a Loremaster? Shouldn't all the real knowledge out there be enough to keep you busy?"

"*Rhrr*, perhaps." Silbadilio's tentacles bunched up into a bit of a defensive posture. "Yet I shudder at the consequences, if ever I were to deal solely in hard facts." He did, in fact, shudder.

Art winced skeptically. "You're gonna have to explain that."

"With pleasure!" He began to pace back and forth through the air, and not in the most elegant fashion... basically proving he wasn't an Angus Dei, either. "Largely, one must trace the seriousness of our convention back to the Great Regression. From time immemorial, it had been taken for granted that the path to true enlightenment was – and certainly ought to be – quite long and exclusive." He slumped in the air. "But, as we all learned from the Regression, the fulfillment of Knowledge is sadly attainable. Within a mere score of years, our forebears had mastered the entire universe, as well as proven that there is naught to do with that mastery, save to destroy ourselves. I daresay, we were never so confused as when we knew everything. Only by providence did we endure that manic time...

"Afterwards, it became clear that we would have to take careful precautions. The pursuit of Knowledge had to be tempered in some way, lest the cosmos fall to a second darkness. It was thus that my folk – the Prosketosa Daffadars – had our path made for us to the very forefront of the intellectual world. We were already quite adept at inventing meaningless absurdity... but never so much as when we were introduced to the greatest possible means to that end: science."

"Science?"

"Oh my, yes. *Bfrlm*! Of course, science was once merely a methodical study of the natural world... truly, the humblest of beginnings. But my people have since advanced the purposes of science by great strides... and vice-versa. For, as we long ago discovered, while science may quickly reach the limits of its practical application, it can also provide a truly inexhaustible resource for baseless fancy, once you get a good handle on the jargon." He turned to Art, flashing seriously. "For instance, did you know that the world actually pre-existed the first Meduselda by several hundred million years, and that we can be quite sure of this because of the rate of decay in certain carbon isotopes?"

Art blinked. "No, I didn't."

"Neither did I, for I have only just made it up! Ha-ha!" he laughed triumphantly. "There now, that was a fine little bit of work! Not bad on a whim, I daresay... *blhr*... but you know, I can do much better, given proper time to think. You should hear this other bit I came up with last week, about the thirty-eight-dimensional squiggles that are the quantum of all matter in the universe. Truly exceptional balderdash, that! And very complicated. I have already forgotten most of it, which only speaks to its quality."

"So..." Art ventured... "...you *have to* make stuff up... to protect everyone from getting too smart?"

Silbadilio inclined himself in the air solemnly. "You begin to glimpse the remarkable importance of what I do here. What *all* Loremasters must do." He outstretched a few tentacles, narrating ceremoniously into the empty middle-ground. "To bury useful facts under a landslide of poppycock... that is our high calling."

Art shrugged. "Your story, Pal."

"*Hrfm*, yes," Silbadilio replied, reengaging. "I could go on, but it seems you were about to ask something else some time ago... is that correct?"

"I was," Art nodded. "I came here in search of answers, Silbadilio." He pointed, leveling a stern look. "*Straight* answers, kapeesh?"

"I make no promises," Silbadilio gave his disclaimer, even as he crossed over to a side room. "This way to the study," he explained, gesturing. "Let us hash out these heavy questions of yours there."

* * *

"Werehumans... *gvrfhml*... Werehumans..." Silbadilio mused aloud for a long interval, making room for a whole string of his guttural noises that weren't quite grumbles, grunts or guffaws, but were nevertheless unmistakably intellectual in nature. Art's gaze began to absently rove over the assorted trinkets in the study while he waited. Most of the Loremaster's belongings were simply shrouded under dustcovers, but among the things left out in the open, he chiefly noted an abacus, a big emerald in a mantle setting atop one of the many bookshelves, a bowling pin, and lastly, a potato that had been run-through with several thin copper filaments.

Each item was snazzy in its own way, but ultimately failed to enhance Art's patience. He listened to the sound of Silbadilio's brainy nothings for thirty seconds tops, before he felt he had to press him...

"That's what I said... *Werehumans.* What do you know about 'em?"

"Oh, quite likely everything... and more," Silbadilio answered. "But *hrf*, I am not so much considering the question you asked... as I am the larger question from which it stems."

Art couldn't quite suppress a tired sigh. "What question is that?"

"The question of the Syzygy itself, my boy. That is: Do Syzygies in fact cause extra-worldly effects? Because, if they don't, then the question of Werehumans is rather moot... at least, for one in your position, who has already expressed a wish for some verity on the matter."

"Okay then," Art nodded. "I'll change my question, if it helps. *How about* Syzygies? Do they really cause funky stuff to happen?"

Silbadilio tipped a pipe at Art, then. "A much better question. And the answer is: *yes.*"

Art felt his heart skip a beat. He scooched up in the deep-backed chair Silbadilio had proffered. "They *do*?" The hair on the back of his neck began to prickle. Though he'd always figured Syzygies were as likely as not to wreak astronomic mayhem, this vague confirmation from a man of science was enough to set him on edge. "What kind of funky stuff?"

Silbadilio's tentacles curled up in a shrug. "It varies from Syzygy to Syzygy. The number of planets involved greatly affects the severity, you understand. But I suspect a worthy answer calls for some visual aid..."

He turned and floated over to a rather large canvas-covered blob on the floor and threw off the dustcover. Art's eyes bugged somewhat at the sight of a huge, intricate orrery – a working model of the cosmos. Silbadilio produced a hand crank from below the wide, circular brass board, inserting it into an unseen shaft. "*Bf-fm*, let's see..." he narrated, as he wound the whole thing a few clicks, making all the little Worlds pivot slightly along their tracks. "We ought to be about... *here*." He stopped his cranking, putting five planets so nearly in line that Art could hardly see any variance at all as he stood and eyeballed the model.

"So now, the math is really quite complex, but in essence, Syzygies are rated by the number of Worlds that line up, on a scale of three to twelve... or, in your own numbers, three to *nine*. Alignments of only two Worlds do not strictly count on the scale, because they are so common that they do not cause any known effects. After all, it is exceptionally rare that one cannot draw a straight line between any two planets. But at any rate, as you can well imagine, Syzygies rated at '3' are the weakest, and '9', the strongest, with a dandy exponential curve running in between."

He pointed at the World in the very center of the orrery. "Here, of course, is Veralas... in general parlance, 'the earth' or 'the world'. It is the focal point of the known universe... but, as we reside here, that should be no great surprise. Even so, I point this out only to give you some idea of the far-reaching implications that a Syzygy can manifest. According to Dynamic Origin Theory, an alignment of all the planets forces the selection of a new World around which the others orbit." He turned to Art with conspicuous intensity. "Can you well imagine? One moment, we are the *Center*... and the next, that distinction goes to some other daft world!"

"Oof," Art commiserated, shaking his head. "That would be bad."

"*Rnf*! Quite so," Silbadilio replied. He shook a tentacle at Art. "You don't know how fortunate we are, my lad. We have had a Level-9 Syzygy only once in the history of creation... after which, we were very lucky to remain the Center. To this day, we don't even know whether to attribute this to divine providence, incumbency bias, or the one-in-nine odds simply playing-out in our favor."

Art shrugged. "Beats me. But I dunno... maybe it was none of that. You did say this 'Dynamic Origin' thing was only a theory, right?"

Silbadilio brushed the comment away. "In science, the term 'theory' is just a polite way of labelling something quite beyond question, even if we are still sorting out the particulars of how it could possibly be true." He tapped on his collar pensively. "Anyway, we are driving away from the point, and not entirely in the direction I intended. No doubt, you are wondering *why* – or rather, *how* – Syzygies manifest the paranormal..." He seemed to consider Art hopefully.

"...Well, not re..."

"But of course you are! Unfortunately, I cannot give you a definite answer, as this remains a divisive subject among the world's academics. Many hypotheses are still being teased out. However, in my extremely proud opinion, I would say the most substantive argument is that the chaos of Syzygies is intrinsically tied to the master of chaos himself: Wxldlr. It has been suggested that the alignment of planets causes something of an extra-cosmic rip current through which his mischievous energies may flow. Naturally, this idea is rather controversial, as Wxldlr himself remains the subject of much controversy and disinformation, even in educated circles. Many cosmologists still cling to the notion that he is a non-entity, but that is not so. Yet even the epistemology of non-entities has many schools of thought, so exactly *how* not-so it is varies..."

"Whoa, now," Art interjected, gesturing for a halt. "You're running at the mouth in all directions, Silbadilio. Can we get to the point of this before my eyes start to glaze over?"

"Probably not," Silbadilio replied. "But *hrmph*, let me see if I might restrain myself to the escalating effects of various Syzygies, beginning at Level 3 and working our way up the scale..."

"I don't even have time for that," Art insisted, checking his new watch to really sell the image. "We're about to have a 5, right? Why not just tell me what we can expect in the next few days?"

"*Huff*," the Loremaster huffed. "Most short-sighted. We'll have another of these to deal with in a few centuries, you know. And anyway, you would be more correct in saying that we are coming to a Level 5.84 Syzygy, given the near-alignment of two other Worlds, which factors into the equation. But very well: Let us examine some of the dreadful symptoms in store for us..." His voice waxed low and grave. Art held his breath...

"First, there will be moderate shifts in our perception and experience of reality. People may wander in and out of sudden chills or hot-flashes. Some will have random fluctuations in visual acuity. Others may experience a dinging in their ears."

"You mean, a *ringing*?"

"I do not. Nor are sight and hearing the only faculties to be affected. Unusual tactile and olfactory sensations are also possible... prickly toes, the smell of burnt sea-cucumbers, etcetera. On top of that, synesthesia has been known to happen, in which case all of these sensory effects would be impossibly mixed up!"

Art half-sighed. "So far it doesn't sound so bad. Kinda like having the flu, really."

"It gets worse," Silbadilio boded. "Things quickly progress from the abnormal to the downright uncanny."

Art tugged at his collar with renewed dread, while his throat prepared to tie itself off. "Such as?"

Even before he continued, Silbadilio's tenor dropped palpably. "The sky may take on unusual casts and shades. Bouts of unusual weather are possible. The odd person will suddenly find that their daily commute runs uphill both ways. Single socks that have been missing for years mysteriously reappear. Sea, air, and land-speed records will be measured by distance instead of time. Individuals with no history of extrasensory perception whatsoever may at whiles catch brief, transcendental glimpses of the very fabric of existence – an allegedly dark, inky, sans-serif sort of scrawling set across unremarkable white planes, by all accounts. Some even experience visions of past lives."

Art grimaced. "*Past lives*? But reincarnation isn't real."

"Of course not!" Silbadilio expounded. "If it were, then seeing into past lives wouldn't be so extraordinary at all, now would it?"

He shrugged. "I guess not."

At this juncture, they came unexpectedly to a beat of silence. Art would've liked to think that Silbadilio had reached the end of his horrific list. But a world-wearied investigator knew better. The Loremaster wasn't finished... oh, no. He was *hesitating*...

Art had to dare himself to get things rolling again...

"...Is there more?"

"Considerably," Silbadilio intoned. "Thus far we have visited only the most rudimentary, *experiential* effects. Now, I fear, we are about to venture into the *transformative*..."

"Transformative... right..." Art repeated uncomfortably. "As in, people turning into Werehumans?"

"*Hrph-hrm*, indeed..." Silbadilio confirmed, bobbing solemnly in the air. "The reverse-lycanthropy you speak of is well within the scope of possibility here. In fact, even were this a much weaker Syzygy, I would not rule it out." He sighed an educated sigh. "Alas that Werehumans are not the only affronts to nature we can anticipate. There are more."

The fact that Art's mission to debunk Werehumans had just imploded on him hardly registered. The word '*more*' was far too open-ended to step away from. "Like what?"

"Well, as a random for-instance, there is Spontaneous Palatal Inversion."

"Spontaneous-What-Now?"

"It is a phenomenon where the tongue detaches from the floor of the mouth and fuses to the roof instead."

"*Bleah*," Art replied.

"Aptly put, I am sure. And yet, the annals of history record many worse anomalies. Panoramic triscopy. Heavy nitrogenic thermal synthesis. Non-linear, inverse-perspective scaling. In some very extreme instances, people and objects have been known to temporarily devolve into planar triangles... or even tiny but macroscopic cells of red, green, and blue light."

By this point, Art's breath was scalding on his tongue... still thankfully un-inverted. "That's terrifying."

"Yet there are graver dangers still. Even the transformative effects fail to top the chart. At this Level, our reality is at intermediate risk of being brutalized by extra-cosmic phenomena."

"What does that even mean?"

"*Brfhrh*!" he exclaimed, throwing his tentacles out in all directions. "The better question by far: What *doesn't* it mean!? Virtually anything could happen! Political primaries are liable to start-up months or years ahead of schedule. Environmentalist groups could succeed in cutting entire nations off from their own energy supplies. The airwaves might be completely overrun by animal rights fundraisers!"

Finally, Art's tension snapped, and he was left in utter bewilderment. "Political primaries? Environmentalist groups? Airwaves and animal rights?"

"Believe me, you don't want to know," Silbadilio explained.

Art slouched and sighed, feeling a strange sort of relief in the idea that the heaviest stuff of this cataclysm-in-progress was somehow beyond his comprehension. "Well... that's an awful load to take in all at once. But at least it'll all blow over in a few days, I guess."

Silbadilio's only response to this remark was a very conspicuous failure to respond.

"Silbadilio?" Art questioned at length. "It *will* blow over in a few days? Right?"

The Meduseldan couldn't help flashing a brooding sort of alarm. "We Loremasters don't usually tell people these sorts of things..." he began slowly, "...but, since you're a detective..."

"What is it?" Art despaired to ask. "What more could there be?"

"Well..." Silbadilio hesitated, before he began to coast over to a window. Art fell in step behind him. When they reached the pane, Silbadilio gestured out into the sky. "Tell me: What do you see out there?"

"The Other Worlds, of course," Art said, feeling as if they'd somehow circled back to the start of the whole conversation.

"*Gph*, yes, but what *about* them?"

Art grew suddenly indignant. "Well, they're lining up. We've been over this."

"Not *that*..." Silbadilio insisted. "You must look *closer*. What else do you see that is abnormal?"

Art searched the Worlds with greater and greater intensity, until his eyes hurt from squinting. "I honestly don't know what I'm looking for," he admitted finally.

"It is the *angle*, my lad! The Worlds are *canted* – turned to the side by not less than 0.0328 degrees! It can be observed in the sun and all the stars as well."

On a second look, Art began to see what he was talking about. The Worlds *were* tipped ever so slightly to one side! Though, personally, he wouldn't have put it anywhere above 0.023 degrees...

"Wow... that's weird," he said. "What does a Loremaster make of it?"

"One of two things," Silbadilio replied. "Either Veralas itself has shifted unaccountably... or else, the entire rest of the universe has! But whichever it is, I may say that it is quite unprecedented. No such planar misalignment has ever been observed before!"

"Jeepers..." Art marveled. "That's gotta be a bad sign, huh?"

"Oh, undoubtedly," Silbadilio agreed. "The worst part is, since we have no precedent to refer back to, and only the most haphazard conceptions of what the root cause could possibly be, there is hardly any knowing *how* bad a sign it is! *However...*" he portended, "...in my estimation, it is not unreasonable to suggest that a new singularity such as this – particularly when paired with another potent cosmic event – may very well herald the final end of all existence as we know it."

Art gaped. "The *End*? Like, of ***everything***?"

Silbadilio approximated a nod. "That is what I'm driving at, yes."

Art struggled to digest these rather broad implications, quickly finding it more agreeable to try to reject the whole idea outright. "I mean... that seems a little over-dramatic for a little 0.0328-degree rotation, don't you think?"

"*Hmp*!" Silbadilio reprimanded him. "Why, silly boy! Don't you know? There is simply no omen too small to kick off an apocalypse!"

Art sighed again – this time, exasperated. "Well, okay. That kinda puts a damper on my plans for the evening." He absently slid his notepad into his pocket and started for the door. "But, I guess I got what I came for... and then some. I have to go now. So thanks, Silbadilio..." He paused a moment, as irony necessitated. "Thanks a lot."

"Any time!" Silbadilio affirmed. "It was my pleasure."

Art had one foot beyond the threshold of the study when he suddenly paused mid-thought, turning slyly back around. "There's just one more thing..." he recited, furrowing a brow.

"Yes?"

"Everything you just told me..." Art specified. "How do I know there's a lick of truth to it? To *any* of it?"

"Importantly, you don't," the Loremaster answered, starting to float after him. "I will see you to the door, my lad – where I may best await the next caller..."

Silbadilio had nearly floated past Art, when he suddenly stopped, and turned to him. "*Hrfv*... there *is* one more thing..." he said quietly.

"Okay," Art reluctantly went along. "Lay it on me."

"You will do well to take heed of the nightfall, my lad. Perhaps it is too obvious to even merit my mentioning, but I mention it all the same. The Syzygy is always most potent at *night*."

* * *

Art was only hazily engaged in the moments that followed – the polite farewells... maneuvering around a Human woman in hat and sunglasses who surprised him at the front door… hearing Silbadilio making some comment about how lively business was today, before the door was shut and Art found himself shuffling down the street. He couldn't help being a bit down in the dumps. Suddenly, he had more to worry about than ever… even though, in essence, he hadn't learned anything at all. Maybe the universe was about to crumble. Maybe it wasn't. Werehumans were real. Unless, of course, they weren't…

Hands huffily stuffed in his pockets, Art left Braintrust Bluff behind him, sure of only one thing:

Deborah was *not* going to let him off the hook tonight.

Chapter 9

Sergeant Paprika wove his way back into the side-streets of the Meduseldan district – a bag of donuts under one arm, and a huge flagon of coffee in the other. As a sergeant, he had the privilege of delegating certain critical errands, such as these supply runs back and forth to burbs that actually sold food and drink. But what with his current assignment – overseeing an extremely boring audit of the Embassy papers – who better to delegate to than himself?

Rounding a final bend in his course, he skirted the edge of a wide square, absently hearing a town crier repeat the same public bulletin he'd been reciting to the jellyfish commuters all afternoon:

"Attention! From the St. Argonsburg Police Department: There has been a recent killing! The suspect remains in custody at present, but we have thus far been unable to identify any victim. Effective immediately, we are broadening the search to include our Meduseldan population. If you – or someone you know – has recently been murdered, you are ordered to report it at once, under penalty of death!"

Paprika just shook his head. With a lame call to action like that, it was all they could do to hope the Meduselda would take the matter seriously...

Finally, he returned to the Dronehood office, relieved to shut out the sky and all its omens for a while. He hardly bothered to dance around the papers strewn everywhere. With a swipe of his arm, he cleared some desk space for the coffee and donuts. And then, before he could even pour or munch on any creature comforts for himself, the swarm began...

"Sergeant Paprika, Sir!" called Corporal Ocelot as he dashed right through piles of documents.

"Hold your horses, Corporal!" Paprika replied. "I brought enough for everybody."

"It's not that, Sir! There's been a development while you were out!"

Paprika's eyes bugged. "Don't tell me you actually found something." It seemed impossible. After the first 17 hours of watching the Clerks, he was sure they'd all agreed: Tweed was a ghost. The Embassy had completely scrubbed him...

"But we did, Sir." The corporal handed his sergeant a nice, officious file. "His name appears on this minute from the reading of a last Will and Testament."

Sure enough, Paprika found the name for himself. "Well, I'll be... 'Arcadian Tweed'," he read aloud, before his eyes dutifully returned to the top of the document... whereupon his heart skipped a beat or two. If he thought the news so far had been astonishing, nothing could have prepared him for what he found there...

"Wait..." he insisted. "Wait-wait-wait. There's no way. Am... am I supposed to believe that Tweed was there for the reading of *this* will? *His* will?!"

"It's there in black and white, Sir."

"But... but that could mean..."

"It very well could."

Paprika steadied himself against the desk, while Ocelot looked on expectantly... eager for an order. Finally, the junior officer's enthusiasm got the best of him...

"Shall we inform Ms. Cordon?"

Paprika shook his head. "I think we're a little further out of our depth now than that. This changes everything. The Czarina *herself* will want to know."

"What do we do, then?" Corporal Jenkins asked, wading into the situation.

Paprika looked up from the minute. "The High Constable's still at Headquarters. We'll see if we can't bring this straight to him."

* * *

"For goodness' sake, Captain, straighten that tie!" Miloje demanded.

"You've already straightened if for me, Sir," Alexei reminded him. "And that was only after the first time you told me to straighten it myself." He eyed his superior quizzically... nervously. "Is his excellency the High Constable something of a fanatic when it comes to ties?"

"I'd rather not find out," Miloje replied, reaching out and improving on his own straightening job. "I have worked under High Constable Dante Amadeus for many years now, and in that time, I've discovered that the less I learn of him, the better I like him."

"How very cryptic, Sir," Alexei said, while Miloje went on to fairly batter him into a better posture. "Is there anything else I should know about him, prior to our first meeting?"

"Well, principally, you must remember that he is a royal, in essence," Miloje explained. "He runs a tighter ship than I do. You know I never had much use for the 'high grammar'... I'd rather have a straight, no-nonsense report from my inferiors. Not so the High Constable. He will expect it. So you'd better warm-up your 'thee's and 'thou's."

The captain nodded. "Right... of course, Sir."

"Besides that, I would urge you to curb your natural enthusiasm," Miloje went on. "He will always prefer the sound of his own voice to yours. If you don't do anything to call attention to yourself, we should all have a good meeting." The Deputy Constable turned an amused look over at Horus. "Everyone but you, that is, Templar. Though, I suppose I should thank you. Your humanitarian inquest into the Grufthoffen Stalag will prove a welcome diversion, I'm sure."

Horus turned up his palms. "Well, I do hope *someone* profits by the attempt. But while we're on the subject of Constable Amadeus, I wonder: What do you think, Milo? How do you rate my odds of convincing the man to turn the denizens of his Stalag loose?"

"Let me see if I can put a positive spin on it," Miloje answered. "You've struck some unlikely bargains in your day, Counselor. This I would not count as the least of them." A sudden thought made the old policeman snap his fingers. "What we really need here is a lint roller."

"I can go get one, Sir," Alexei offered.

"I'll come with you," Horus blurted, abruptly noticing a window of opportunity to council the captain and pouncing on it before his powers of discretion could catch up. Miloje studied him dubiously...

"What for?" he asked with narrow eyes. "Does it indeed take two of you to complete such a daunting task?"

"Well..." Horus began, finding no words to try. "I thought... that is..."

"Oh, never mind," Miloje sighed. "If you would have words alone, you need only say so. I'll go get the silly thing myself." And with that, he was gone.

The room was silent for a beat. Then, Alexei turned to Horus. "Does the Deputy Constable speak rightly, Mr. Templar? Is there something troubling you that I might help with?"

Horus chuckled. "That's precisely what I meant to ask *you*, Alexei. It's understood that you've been under a lot of added pressure lately. *Marital* pressure, if I don't miss my guess."

Alexei balled one hand up in front of his face, picking at his teeth for a moment. "You cut right to the heart of things at times, don't you, Sir? I'm alarmed to learn I haven't kept up appearances so well as I thought. Evidently, I am the subject of some gossip... or what may be worse." He searched Horus with a worried look. "How much do you know?"

"Only what I've already ventured," Horus replied. "What's the matter, Alexei? Is your new wife really so abrasive?"

The captain shook his head. "On the contrary... I consider her to be quite lovely in most respects. A tad on the inquisitive side, perhaps, but that is surely second nature for a..." The end of his sentence hit the ground with a proverbial 'thump' as he dropped it.

Much as he was butting into personal business, Horus was quite invested now. He didn't do much to hide it, either. "What, Alexei? Second nature for a what?"

Alexei eyed the doorway. He went so far as to peek out and check the hall. And even with the coast clear, he was careful to keep his voice down...

"What you ask is privileged information, which must not be repeated without my say-so. The truth may shock you, as it certainly did me. But I have since come to terms with it... it is merely the accident of her profession, which of course, she had no say in... no more than you or I. Thus, she cannot be held wholly accountable for the atrocities she must commit, in her line of work..."

Horus' brows knit. "What line of work is that? What does she do that's so heinous? Go on... you can tell me."

Alexei's whole face scrunched. His eyes were buried in deep folds... his lip quivered as he bit down on it, looking at once as if he was straining with all his might both to force the horrible words out, and also keep them in...

"She's... a *reporter*."

Horus blanched. "A reporter?" He reeled, grappling with a deeper sympathy than he'd known in some months. "Alexei, I'm... I'm so sorry."

"No, Mr. Templar, you mustn't apologize!" Alexei assured him. "Once again, I am in your debt. I have had no one to confide in, these last few days... no one I could trust with this highly compromising information. I can't imagine the consequences, if my coworkers were to find out. I cannot even write home about her! Especially right now, what with all the controversy the news has been stirring up about the Syzygy."

Horus reflexively laughed it off. "Tweed showed me some of the recent headlines. But surely no one is putting any real stock in them."

Alexei replied only with a look.

Horus cleared his throat. "...I take it they *are*?"

"We've had a dramatic influx of dubious reports in the last 21 hours. Alleged UFO sightings, apparitions trapped in attics... as if we have any protocol for such things. We even had one fellow report that his neighbor had transformed himself into a stack of polygons."

Again, Horus could do little more than stare. "I... I had no idea. Though, looking back, I suppose the signs of mass paranoia were all there. When I went out last night, the people were – shall we say – a bit on the fidgety side?"

"And it's likely to get worse as the Syzygy progresses," Alexei replied, nodding. "But that is not the worst of it, Mr. Templar. I begin to suspect that my wife is no idle player in this media blitz. From nearly the words, 'I do,' she has been asking many questions about the Tweed investigation, and those assigned to it. I would have preferred not to answer any of them, of course, but she insisted I must, on the grounds that there should be no secrecy in marriage. Even now, I believe, she is on the tail of some private detective or other working the case." He shook his head dejectedly. "My own beloved... the enemy of civic order. How shall I ever live with myself?"

"Not by resolving to keep it a secret from your family and coworkers, I suggest," Horus ventured. "As you said, it wasn't her choice to become a reporter, any more than it was your choice to marry her." Alexei started to say something, but Horus stopped him with an upraised hand. "Now, I know: In this world, having no choice is no excuse. But being married to a journalist... it's a fact of your life now. And – I would argue – the sooner you face whatever consequences come of it, the better."

Alexei mulled it over, appearing to find at least a little comfort in having some insights to weigh beside his own. "I do not take your advice lightly, Sir... I am sure it is founded in wisdom. Even so, I think I shall wait... at least until this Syzygy has blown over. You'll appreciate that this isn't exactly the best time, won't you? Surely there is no sense in incriminating myself now, when tensions are already at their peak."

"I suppose not," Horus admitted grudgingly. "But whatever you do, don't find yourself making one excuse after another to put this off. Matters of the heart must be faced, not endlessly postponed. That would be the most senseless thing of all." He delivered this final bit of counsel with charismatic confidence, unaware of even a trace of irony.

"Thank you, Mr. Templar. I will certainly do my best."

Before too much silence could intervene, there was a deliberate sound of footsteps in the hall. Miloje reappeared soon after...

"Good timing, Milo," Horus said. "We were just concluding our business."

"Not such good timing as I would've liked," the old policeman replied. "There is no time left for lint-rolling. We must see the High Constable *now*."

* * *

The room was bleak – colorless. They stood arrayed around the desk that – on any other day – would have been Blackforest's, each masking private flutters with stern fronts. Absently, they heard the scribe's pen scratching away. Actively, they watched the back of the High Constable's head, while he gazed out through Hamilton's blinders into stark, white nothingness.

Horus ticked off the silent minutes in his head, feeling a feisty sense of contempt steadily rise as the scene unfolded. This 'meeting' with the Constable had so far amounted to his simply being let into the room, without the back of Amadeus' head taking any apparent notice. There had been no introductions. There had been no *speaking.* Only the dratted pen. By this time, Horus had no remaining expectation of having his business announced. It seemed doubtful that even Alexei would be properly introduced to his future boss. No one was in any hurry to step up and disturb the Constable's ruminations. No one *dared*...

But then, as much as it irked Horus to see Miloje and Blackforest so cowed, he could hardly blame them. The High Constable was the supreme office in the land over both the military and law enforcement. He answered only to the Czarina herself, and he roughly approximated her reputation for kindheartedness. The laws of self-preservation dictated that this was not the sort of man whose attention you would actively seek, if he was content to ignore you...

Though, perhaps it was the High Constable's distant air that really bothered Horus most. It wasn't merely inconvenient... it was vexing... *puzzling*, even. *Why* was he ignoring them? Was this just his way of lording it over? Horus' instincts suggested otherwise. He was, after all, of a species which could smell fear. And, while he couldn't be sure, he had a distinct sense that he was getting a whiff of it now... and not just what was coming from his SAPD counterparts...

With a last flourish, the pen finally came to rest. "Tis finishèd, my liege," the scribe announced, with all the confidence of a hen in a fox house. He attempted to hand the papers off to Amadeus...

"What? Oh," the High Constable replied, before waving his aide away. "That's fine... just hand it off to one of them."

The scribe blanched. "W...which one, Lord High Constable?"

"What makes you think I care?" he asked. "I shouldn't have to tell you not to bother me with trifles when I'm busy. Just get it done and get yourself back up the mountain."

"Yes... of courseth, Sir." The scribe flung the report into Blackforest's hands and promptly marched through the door.

After the flurry of activity, Blackforest unjumbled the papers, eyeing them dubiously. "This... this is your report, High Constable?"

Amadeus' heretofore stationary head actually turned back a few degrees. "Is this a day for stupid questions?" he retorted. "You have it in your hands, Blackforest. Does it *look* like my report?"

"Why yes, of course it does," Blackforest snickered. Horus was surprised. He knew his old rival's snickers, and while this one was certainly nervous, it was also a bit toothy. "I only ask because I noticed your scribe didn't take so much of a word of actual dictation."

The High Constable's hand flopped dismissively. "It's not like this is Henry's first PD audit. I'm sure he was able to convey my expectations well enough."

"I should say he was," Blackforest said, flipping to the last page. "In the essay field – marked 'Areas Where Improvement will be Expected by Next Audit' – he simply wrote, 'A lot.'"

"You see? My thoughts exactly. Now are we quite done here?"

Miloje cleared his throat. "There art an order of business which remaineth unaddressed, Sir. Tis the matter of my replacement. I hath brought him forth that thou shoulds't be introduced unto him."

"Ah, right... I forgot," the High Constable admitted. "I heard you were planning on bugging-out soon." He snapped his fingers, trying to jog his memory. "It was some sort of heart thing? Now I don't remember."

Horus watched Miloje's mustache furrow. "Actually... that malady dost no longer troubleth my person... Sir."

"Well, how nice for you. Still, you really *are* getting up there. You're bound to keel-over from something or other pretty soon. So sure. Introduce me to this... what's his name?"

"Alexei, O greatly esteemed High Constable," Alexei answered on his own behalf.

"Alexei? Alexei, *what*?"

"...I...?" the Captain replied, tensely knotting his fingers. "...I doth faileth to grasp the question, Lord."

The High Constable looked over his shoulder, but his bald head was only a dark profile in the slitted light of the window. "Your last name, Son. Surely you have one?"

"I... I do not, my liege."

"Well get one, then. The office of Deputy Constable is much too high for any man to fill with only his birthname."

Alexei nodded deeply. "It will be done as thou hast command-eth-ed, High Constable."

"Very good. Then I think we're done here." He waved them all off. "Leave me to my office. I'd like some peace and quiet before I return to the Palace."

"But we're *not* done," Horus interjected, even as everyone else began to turn away. "I also have a matter to bring before you. A matter of some urgency."

The room was still, then. Quiet. So quiet, in fact, that Horus distinctly heard a pin drop... though he had no idea where in all the wide world that pin might be...

High Constable Amadeus swiveled in Blackforest's chair. As a man of great military prominence, his bottom lip was always puffed out – over-inflated with the true spirit of being perpetually unimpressed – but his other, rectangular features managed to take on a specially uninspired cast. He eyed Horus for a goodly interval. Then, he turned to Hamilton...

"Who is this man?"

"I'm Horus Templar," Horus asserted, "a Public Defender for the city of St. Argonsburg."

Amadeus sat back. "Horus Templar," he repeated, suddenly losing his air... looking deviously amused. "I've heard of you. You're the one who got the Czarina to let Public Enemy Number One walk. Must be you think that makes you somebody."

"Not really," Horus shrugged. "But I've learned to take risks when it's important."

Amadeus huffed. "How nice to know that barging into a confidential department audit and demanding my time still rates as 'risky'." He folded his arms. "What do you want?"

"Simply, I've come to ask that you give the Grufthoffen Stalag a second thought."

It was subtle, but Horus was sure he saw the High Constable's eyes flare for a fraction of a second. Less subtle by far, the smell of fear washed over the office afresh...

"The Grufthoffen Stalag? What about it?"

"The prisoners there... our own soldiers," Horus explained. "I've been to the Stalag. I've seen the way these men are being misused myself. They have served the State in the very highest capacity... and in turn, the State has elected to turn a meager profit for their captivity. These are *your* men, High Constable. Men who would gratefully serve again, if you would only ransom them. And this would seem to be the opportune time to do so. The Despotopians have their own Kaiser to ransom. Why not make the inmates of Grufthoffen part of the bargain? Surely, it would be better for you than letting able-bodied troops molder behind a stockade."

Horus was met with no response... only a look of astonishment. The High Constable appeared to be frozen. In all that awkward silence, the only thing Horus could think to do was shore-up his argument...

"...Mind you, they'd only be *part* of the bargain. I'm sure the Czarina intends to collect a massive fee for the Kaiser, as is her right. But I would argue that the extradition of your men is worth... a *modest* discount, at least..."

Amadeus remained speechless. But at last, his jaw set. He heaved a deep breath through his nose. And then, he stood...

"What I'm about to say does not leave this room," he explained. Horus wasn't sure anyone so much as nodded, but their compliance was instinctively felt. "There isn't going to be any ransom for the Kaiser," Amadeus went on. "Not in point of fact."

Horus' eyes bugged. "But... surely you don't mean the Czarina plans to usurp the Despotopian throne? The Inquisition doesn't tend..."

The High Constable cut him off with an upraised hand. "Don't bother leaping to any wild conclusions; just let me finish. As far as the *Czarina* is concerned, the deal is still being struck." At this juncture, he swallowed dryly. "There's... something she doesn't know. Something she must *never* know."

This was some kind of revelation they'd stumbled on. Neither Horus, nor anyone in the room, particularly fancied knowing something the Czarina could *never* know. But, at the same time, it was the most compelling inside information any of them had ever been offered. The most compelling by far...

"What is it?" Horus asked.

"It's the *Kaiser,*" Amadeus revealed, sounding deeply haunted. "I can't ransom him, because I don't *have* him. Not anymore. He escaped."

Suddenly, it all made perfect sense. Kaiser Hienrechenshlagen's capture had been the toast of the entire nation for weeks, and certainly not the least in the Czarina's circles. She was naturally expecting a king's fee for the return of the Despotopian sovereign. That the High Constable had since botched the windfall of the century would come as no small disappointment, if the Czarina were to find out. And, in that instance, it was clear that Amadeus stood to be more disappointed than anyone. After all, even a High Constable's head could come suddenly detached, under the right circumstances...

"*Creators save us,*" Blackforest swore. "To think of the Despotopians... pulling off a raid like that."

Amadeus shook his head. "No, it didn't go down that way; you don't understand. I only wish there *had* been some sort of counterattack. Maybe *that* I could've explained. The truth... the *real* truth... it's frankly incredible. Almost unbelievable..." He paused, searching for words, or else the resolution to say them. "Hienrechenshlagen wasn't rescued. He *let himself out...*"

Horus grimaced. The High Constable was right: The truth – if it *was* the truth – was not to be believed. "He escaped single-handedly? How could that be? Was he not adequately guarded?"

"*Adequate*?" Amadeus asked contemptuously. "You want to talk about 'adequate'? We had him penned-in behind a whole division! That rates as 'adequate' by any traditional stretch of the imagination. But how could we expect that..." He gave up midsentence, electing instead to cover his mouth with his fist and look studiously away. "They said he used *magic*. They said he had moves like nobody's seen since Carlos Washoe. Maybe it sounds like a lame excuse to you, but I believe them. And it's more than just the scorch marks he left all over the inside of the fortress." He shook his head, bit his lip. "The war was still in its infancy. They even had some early victories that really shook us. There was never any sense in him leading from the front the way he did... putting himself out there, right where we could nab him. Why... why would he do that? It was... it was almost as if..."

Horus waited in vain for him to finish his statement. "You think he meant to be captured?"

He nodded. "That *is* what I think."

"But why? Why be captured, only to gamble on an escape of long odds?"

"I don't know," Amadeus admitted. "Maybe it was a bold stunt to end the war quickly. Or maybe he was sending us a message. A message that'll be the death of me, if it gets out..."

"What sort of message?"

"That things are changing," he boded. "Getting away from us. Wandering into uncharted waters. Take that trade war with Maenea last year. We never really accounted for that one. Or how about the Twin Queens? Or the long silence overseas? Granted, those things've been going on for a while now, but it doesn't change the fact that no one can explain them. And what about magic? Where did *that* come from? What's it going to mean for the future... especially if the Kaiser can leverage it to get a leg up? Maybe he already has..."

Horus shrugged. "I wouldn't spend too much time trying to make all the dots connect if I were you, High Constable. The world has its oddities... I don't think it's best to lop them all together into one nameless fear."

Amadeus nodded. "You could be right, Templar. I hope you are. But either way, I think we've lost a step. The fact of the matter is, we didn't win this war, even if Hienrechenshlagen lost it. He handed us the victory, then denied us the glory. He lost on *his* terms. That's never happened before. And it has me shaken."

"Well, that's certainly alarming in its own right," Blackforest interjected. "But unless I missed something, you have a bigger problem. A more *immediate* one, anyway. How can you hope to keep the Czarina from learning what really happened?"

"I have a solution," Amadeus assured him. "It's simple, but far from painless. I'm just going to have to pay the Kaiser's supposed ransom out of my own pocket."

Horus fiddled with the hairs on his chin. "Interesting. I suppose the main problem will be in making sure the money can't be traced back to you."

"That's no trouble at all. The Czarina won't even stop to question which direction the coffers are filled from. The real trick is coming up with enough funds. Sure, I can float the annual GDP of Despotopia a couple times over, but it wouldn't leave much to live on for a while. What I need is a clever angle to mitigate the expense…" His gaze singled Horus out again. "So how about it, Horus Templar? Can you get me out of this fix?"

"Me?!" Horus fairly protested. "You want *my* help?"

"What do you think I just told you all these compromising secrets for? My health? Yes, I want *your* help. You're the one that just proposed a 'prisoner exchange' as a part of the overall ransom. More than that: You packaged it with all that flowery nonsense about honor and patriotism and whatnot." He shook his head. "I couldn't write a speech like that to save my life. But you rattled it right off like it wasn't even rehearsed. I know phony appeals to virtue are part of the territory for a lawyer, but I even half believed you meant it."

Horus shrugged off the man's ugly presumptions uncomfortably. "One of my more inspired moments, I suppose."

"Well, it was a fine time for showmanship. I'm convinced you're just the man to broker your prisoner exchange… and save me a nest egg in the process. I want you to write it all up for me. Make the best case you can for it." He snapped his fingers. "Heck, write a speech and put your name on it! Why shouldn't you get credit for your good deed, after all?"

Horus saw right through this ploy. "Especially if it provides you with an expedient scapegoat… in the likely event the Czarina would've rather had the extra cash," he ventured.

At this, Blackforest went slack-jawed.

But the High Constable only grinned mischievously. "Well, so long as we understand each other." He held out his hand. "So how about it, Horus?"

Horus eyed the hand as if he might dirty his sleeve if he didn't grab it carefully. But he reached out and shook on it. "Why not? Lest I forget, I *did* ask for this."

Amadeus nodded as they concluded their shake. "You may not be sorry. In fact, I think this could be an important turning point in your career. No doubt, a man like you could use a friend in the State…"

"I wouldn't know about any alleged 'friendship'," Horus came back. "As far as I'm concerned, this is just a spot of good business."

Finally, Amadeus' face resumed its surly disposition. "Have it how you like, Horus. But here's a little friendly advice just the same: Be careful what you say around your betters. Or one day, one of us might just get the feeling you don't respect him very much."

Horus dared a grin. "So long as we understand each other."

Chapter 10

"Some times, Horus... some times..." Blackforest kept portending as they wound through the torchlit halls of Civil Headquarters, failing to note the seemingly unimportant detail of Sgt. Paprika heading the way they'd come.

"Sometimes what, Hamilton?" asked Horus.

"Sometimes I think you should have your head examined... before somebody gets the idea to send it rolling off your shoulders."

"There was never any danger," Horus assured him. "Not after the deal was struck, at any rate. The High Constable made it clear he was depending on me to get him out of a major bind. Why should I pretend to feel that he was owed any homage?"

"Because he *is*, Horus. Or anyway, his office is."

"Do *you* respect him, Hamilton?" Horus deflected.

"Of course I don't," he answered. "But at least I know better than to admit it to his face."

"I'm not sure what choice he left me," Horus argued. "Granted, he's up against a lot right now, but that hardly excuses anything I saw in there. He obviously feigned your entire audit, which was his responsibility. He paid no mind to the plight of his own soldiers... besides saving him money, he obviously felt the whole ransom idea was a joke. He even impugned the very idea of honor. And if all that wasn't enough, in the end he tried to make it out like he'd bought me off. Something had to be said to let him know: One deal doesn't mean he has me in his back pocket."

"I have to admit, it was nice seeing Amadeus get egg on his face." Blackforest laughed. "Who knows? Maybe this debacle with the Kaiser is just the reckoning he needs to shape-up a bit. He's on thin ice, and he knows it. And, at the end of the day, he's just as expendable as we are. I say let it be a lesson to him."

Horus shook his head. "I don't get the feeling he's learned any lesson. In fact, I'm afraid a man like him would do almost anything to avoid a lesson like that. Perhaps that's what bothers me most about all this, in the end: I'm enabling him, even if it *is* for the greater good. I only hope we don't come to regret being accessories in Amadeus' big coverup."

"Well thank you for that lovely omen, O great Allseer," Blackforest sneered. "You can count yourself an accessory if you want. Me, I aim to forget everything I heard in there, and the sooner the better. Although..."

Horus turned and appraised his counterpart. "Although what? Is there something he said that particularly troubles you?"

"As a matter of fact, yes," Blackforest admitted. "Horus, does it alarm you at all to think he might be right? About the Kaiser, and Despotopia? About what it could mean, if they really are getting ahead of us somehow?"

Horus grinned. "I didn't think you believed in fairytales, Hamilton. No doubt the High Constable's only nursing his gross incompetence with a fish story... one that's grown larger and larger each time he's rehearsed it. Anyway, I wouldn't let visions of a new era of Despotopian conquest keep you up at night. We have enough real problems on our hands."

"Problems like *Tweed*," Blackforest recited darkly. "Do you have any more ideas on that front?"

"I do." Horus nodded forward, both in salutation and to direct Hamilton's attention. "Here's someone who may be of help now..."

Just then, Deborah arrived in their midst. "Well then... looks like we all came away from our meetings a little the worse for wear," she said.

Horus and Blackforest only exchanged a wide-eyed look. "If you could've been a fly on the wall for the heart-to-hearts I've just had," Horus remarked finally.

"Oh?" she intoned. "Did I miss some juicy gossip?"

"It was choice, to say the least."

"How about the mission itself?"

"An unexpected success. Though it may yet hinge on some persuasive writing."

Blackforest made a show of looking at his timepiece. "If you'll excuse me Ms. Boulevard... Horus. I have other things." He began to walk away with an impatient wave. "Find me when you crack this Tweed case open."

They had no reply for him before he was gone, so they returned to each other.

"What about you?" Horus asked. "Do I dare ask about *your* meeting?"

Deborah shrugged. "It wasn't all bad. At one point he even complimented me on my highly-evolved sense of ambifacient precession."

Horus made a face. "What does that mean?"

"Well, it's Tweed we're talking about, so probably nothing. Although, it might've been something he borrowed out of that technical journal he was reading."

"Technical journal?"

She went shuffling through her handbag. "I have it here, if you want to see it. And you *will* want to see it. It's got what you asked for... the best I could get it."

Once she handed him the journal, he instinctively opened it to a dog-eared page, scanning. What he found was considerably less than what he'd hoped, but it was something...

"*Archy*," he read aloud. "You got him to sign one of these drafts?"

"He practically insisted."

For no real reason, Horus found himself scanning the header on the adjoining page, detailing the function and design of some strange piece of equipment he'd never heard of. The credit for the draft was left blank.

"Deborah... this – whatever it is – was drafted anonymously." He eyed her dubiously, as he seemed to find himself doing over and over in the brief course of this conversation. "Do you think our Tweed is into writing technical manuscripts?"

She shook her head. "I wondered the same thing, so I asked him. He said if he was going to write anything, it would be books. Even though he also made a point to tell me he's never read a book in his life... particularly not the one we're in right now."

Horus gave his most doubtful look of all.

But then, his face and posture softened. "Well, at any rate, I'm sorry to subject you to his nonsense. But once I got the idea to try and collect something in his handwriting, it seemed the expedient thing."

She waved it off. "Being your go-between is all in the line of duty, isn't it? Besides, it was really no trouble. Things have been so crazy lately, what's a little more craziness?"

Horus chuckled. "Things've been crazy, have they? I'm not sure what you mean by that."

"Well, never mind," she sighed. "You've got your hand-written note. I'm sorry if it's much too brief to be any good, but it's really all I could get out of him."

Horus returned unhopeful eyes to the journal. "There *is* rather a shortage of lines to read between here," he admitted. "But Lias Creevey's art is a peculiar one. I don't doubt he can make something of it yet."

"You're too kind," she retorted. "Still, I hope you're right. Shall I meet you back at the office?"

He shrugged. "You could just as easily come with me to see Creevey."

"Do you *need* me there?" she asked.

The question rather surprised Horus. “I don’t expect to… no. Is there something else you need to do?”

“Not really. But I thought I might try to find Art, if there was nothing pressing.”

He grinned weakly. “That’s no trouble. Go ahead.”

She returned his weak grin. “Thanks, Boss. Good luck with your graphologist.”

“Good luck to you, finding Art,” he replied, a little unsure.

As she nodded and walked away, Horus took a moment to try and give form to his sudden doubt. He could tell that Deborah was still feeling poorly in her nondescript way, for which he remained sympathetic. But now he was reminded of her strange propensity of late for seeking Art out. Did these two pieces fit together somehow? Could it be that Deborah was in some fix… some dilemma she’d entrusted to Art, but not to him? They’d all been friends for a long time… but Horus may have taken it for granted that she trusted him at least as much as she trusted Art. Could it be that he was wrong?

Horus shook himself out of such questions. He was thinking childishly… almost jealously. Best to focus on the task at hand. It was time to seek out Dr. Creevey…

* * *

“I think it would look better a little further to the left,” Milt Lias Creevey remarked, chin couched in a contemplative pose. “What do you think, Horus?”

“Oh, undoubtedly,” Horus agreed readily, just as if he was really thinking about the décor. True, in a sense, that *was* what he was thinking about, but not because he had any opinion. Rather, he was curious how the lowly department graphologist had ever arrived in this unlikely role of directing the exact placement of lavish furnishings in a third-story office. The revelation that this office now *belonged* to Creevey scarcely sufficed to explain it. If anything, that was far and away the most perplexing part…

“You’ve really been moving up in the world since last we met, Lias,” Horus said, commencing his leading remarks.

Creevey nodded. “An authentic Murée is nothing to sneeze at,” he replied, evidently of the mind that Horus was only commenting on the portrait, even as the servants continued to finesse it along the wall. “I would've greatly preferred a Finkmeyer or Kaslov, but of course, I'm not one to refuse any of life's finer things, if they happen to come my way."

"So they have been," Horus nodded. "Three offices and three floors in as many months, I'm told. And you can't have won much of that glory from helping me with the little case of Rythigaar the Inquisitor. Must be you've leant a hand in a few capers since then? Some of greater import to the department, no doubt?"

"Well, not so many as you might think," Creevey chuckled with practiced humility. "But you know, a little goes a long way, sometimes." He turned to another servant with a bergère. "Set that over in the corner, would you?"

"Well suffice it to say, your progress is... *impressive*," Horus continued. He considered Creevey himself. The man was in such high spirits that Horus' rather obvious insinuations didn't appear to trouble him at all. He just kept roving over his new office with happy eyes, grinning like a Czar might do on the day of his coronation...

"I might add..." Horus ventured even further, "...that it's rather refreshing to see a little joy around Civil Headquarters. Things have been all doom and gloom ever since the audit was announced."

Creevey shrugged. "Some people are just pessimists. I'm not worried."

"No? You're not the least concerned that something compromising could've been discovered?"

"Audits turn up all sorts of things; that's a known fact," said Creevey, still undaunted. If anything, he seemed more pleased with himself than ever. "Anyway, the verdict's in, and I don't see anyone coming to cart me off. Unless that's why *you're* here."

"Nothing like that," Horus replied, knowing he'd been bested. Whether out of professionalism or wily self-defense, Creevey had put Horus' fishing expedition to rest. He would have to state his business now, and be on with it...

"I have a job for you, Lias," Horus went on. "Another bit of handwriting from a client to decode."

"Ah, *yes*," Creevey said, rubbing his hands together with a devious eagerness. "I was hoping I might get in on this Syzygy Killer case."

"I do wish everyone would stop calling him that," Horus lamented, even as he produced the journal. "See what you can make of this, will you? I do regret it's all I can offer presently."

Creevey squinted at the page he was shown. "A signature, I see? Interesting... very interesting..."

"I'm sorry... I know it isn't much to go on."

The graphologist turned up his palms as he sat the journal on his nice new desk. "There *are* more telling indicators than just volume, Horus. If anything, it's a shame you couldn't get me something shorter."

Horus made no sign... he honestly couldn't tell if Creevey was being sarcastic or not.

Either way, the graphologist worked his loupe up and down those five letters, frowning more and more as he went. "Hm. I guess I wasn't thinking straight when I had a mind to be part of this, Horus."

"Something wrong?"

"Well, as I find myself having to explain a lot lately: I'm a PhD in graphology, not abnormal psychology. This man's head is a real mess. Heavy on the case... *veeeery* light on the basket."

"I see," Horus remarked, trying not to sound too disappointed as he waxed gravely thoughtful. "Still, that's not nothing. At least that suggests the craziness isn't a misbegotten act."

"I should say not," Creevey quipped, pointing where he looked on the signature. "Look at the almost concave tail on the front of this 'h'. If that doesn't scream raging psychopath, I don't know what does." He turned his gaze up to Horus. "What exactly were you *hoping* to find? Maybe there's some trace of it here, if I know what I'm looking for..."

Horus shook his head. "If you can't be sure on your own, I'd rather not say. It seems hardly better than leading a witness."

"Lead away," Creevey invited him. "That is, if you want to walk away with anything useful. I need some fixture to navigate by in this ocean of madness."

Horus sighed. "Well, alright... it's not like I have an abundance of other options at this point. I was hoping you could find a *name*... the name of his victim."

"The *big* question," Creevey nodded. "That's what I was afraid of."

This was far from what Horus wanted to hear. "You don't think you can find it?"

"I'm sure I can't!" Creevey flatly admitted, holding the journal up. "The only name I can find in here is 'Brenda'... but you can plainly see from the heavy gauge at the start of the second two letters that she must've been his schoolmarm, and that she died a long time ago on a retirement holiday to the Neru Gardens."

It was a great disappointment. Horus could only rest his hand on his head, running it slowly over his ears. "I might've known. Why did I ever let myself believe it could really be as simple as walking in here and asking you to divine his great secret?"

"*Well...*" Creevey intoned, letting the word marinate for a while in the air. "...There *is* a great secret here. Something he hasn't told you. Something he never means to tell anyone... or I've forgotten everything I ever learned about the upward slant at the end of a terminal 'y'."

Horus' ears snapped back up. "But not *our* secret? Not the secret of whom he killed?"

"It *can't* be," Creevey answered. "To put it in syntactical terms, this secret of his has no object. It's not anchored to any *one* or any *thing*. A killing could never read this way. So it *has* to be something else."

Horus pressed the operative question. "But what could it be, then? What *is* the secret?"

Creevey shook his head. "I don't know."

Chapter 11

"Maybe we should split up," Deborah suggested. "I could always write the speech for you, if he finds you first... get it outlined, at least. Of course, if he finds me, you're in the clear for the next twelve hours or so. And this way, you won't even have to feel like you sacrificed me for the greater good. It'll just be luck of the draw."

"I think we should just walk right in and explain that we have work to do," Horus countered. "We can't resort to sneaking into our own offices forever. Sooner or later he's just going to have to accept that there are boundaries... that he can't engage us in conversation 21-7. We all have to face this thing like adults."

"Horus, he is *waaay* past being an adult at this point. He's more like a force of nature. You can't reason with him. You'll only get a long, *slow* lecture-series for your trouble."

Horus shook his head. "There's a right way to handle this, Deborah. That means we should try it." He almost gulped. "We have to."

"*Oh-kay*," she sighed. "Don't say I didn't warn you. But whatever we do, let's hop to it... and get out of this dratted cold." She shivered.

"Strange," Horus remarked. "It *is* very chilly out, isn't it? Much too chilly for this time of year. But I could swear I was uncomfortably hot, just a minute ago..."

"No time for puzzling," Deborah urged him, starting to rub her forearms. "I'd rather face death by talking than stay out here another minute."

"Alright," Horus resolved. And with his affirmation, they drew up on the dreaded train car. But even before they might've thought better of it and veered left or right into the cover of darkness, the car's back door opened, and out came a rather flustered-looking Eb Thalymus...

"Well, there y'all are! I was jist about fixin' ta send the po-po's out lookin' for the two o' yous! I do declare: How is we s'posed ta get anythin' done if yer gonna be out galivantin' all day long?"

"Hello, Eb," Horus replied, all a nervous smile. "I'm sorry if you waited up for us. But it's funny you should mention getting things done... as it happens, Deborah and I have quite a bit of work to do at the moment, and can't spare...

"*Work*!? Well, why didn't ya say so?!" Eb asked, clapping his sudden excitement. "Hop right on in and let's git to it!"

They exchanged a look. Then, as if on their final march, they followed Eb inside...

* * *

"Ya gotta start at the start... thet's what I say," Eb explained, well into the second hour of a meandering lecture that had grown seamlessly out of a call to swift action he'd made himself. "Too many times I seen youngins assume facts not yet in evidence, an' leap right inta the middle o' things. Ain't never once worked out. Ya really gotta know what's what b'fore ya can git anyplace! Ya can't take nothin' for granted... thet's for shore."

Sitting in a slouch without hope, Horus noticed a short pause... like a single drop of dew in a vast desert. But "..." was all he managed to say before the next point began...

"Course they's some cases as gits so strange, y'can't hardly tell up from down. Naw, I know y've had some weird ones yerself, Horus, but believe you me, it gits weirder. Why, did I ever tell ya 'bout the time I had ta represent a *pocket telescope* in a civil lawsuit?!"

Horus briefly entertained the notion of truthfully answering, 'Yes, about fourteen times by now.' But of course, his manners got the best of him. "Actually, I think you might've..."

"Naw that was a knock-down drag-out of a thing," Eb laughed nostalgically, just as he had all the other times. "Won a lot of acclaim fer thet one; helped hash-out some important precedents fer proper jurisprudence, when one or more parties is an inanimate object." He leaned forward squinting as his eyes began to survey his car. "I still got my client 'round here someplace. Judge gave me the thing as a keepsake." He got up, quickly checking a few storage cabinets at eye-level. "Naw where'd I put that confounded thing?" He turned away from them, leaning into a lower cabinet. "I think maybe I got it somewhere in the back here..."

A desperate gambit occurred. Horus looked at Deborah, who instinctively looked back at the same moment. He waved her emphatically in his direction, even as he silently stood from his own seat and began to backpedal for the door. With equal stealth, she leapt up and met him in the doorway...

"...Wish I could find time for organizin' all this junk..." they heard Eb remark distantly as he went on rummaging. "Woo-ee! I ain't seen this contraption in a spell. I r'member it plain as day... this here was the critical piece o' evidence in the case o' the gallopin' gallimimus! Or was it the case o' the ombudsman's umbrella? *Heeey*, now looky here! I plum forgot about this one!"

Quiet as can be, Horus nudged the door open. They cracked it only far enough to slip out, then closed it with equal care. They held their breath for a moment, fearing the worst. But after a few anxious seconds passed, and no sound came from within the car to chase them down, they sighed their relief, bounding into Horus' office...

"So this is how adults handle a situation, huh, Boss?" Deborah beamed after they'd shut out the world.

"They say 'never send a boy to do a man's job'," Horus remarked, trying to catch his breath. "I begin to wonder if that works both ways."

"This is really no solution," she almost giggled, still giddy from the absurdity of their flight. "When he finds out we ghosted him..."

"There could be hours of narrating his search of the cabinets before that happens," he supposed. "Let's try and get some work done in the meantime."

* * *

"So how *did* you manage to convince High Constable Dante Amadeus to go along with this idea of yours?" Deborah asked as she sat down to one of her typewriters.

"That's a loaded question. I don't think I can offer any answer that wouldn't be a breach of trust," Horus replied.

"Come on, Boss," she verbally nudged him. "Legal secretaries are exempt from all that confidentiality red tape – you know that."

"But Amadeus isn't a client. And anyway, the less you know, the safer you are."

"*Ugh*, you're only making it worse," she replied, setting a sheet into the paper table. "Sudden danger and intrigue – state-level secrets – and me without a guess..." Horus happened to note her brow furrow, like she was struck with a sudden, unpleasant thought. "Does it have anything to do with the Syzygy?" she asked, in a somewhat lower register than usual.

He chuckled. "The Syzygy? Now where would you get an idea like that? You must be reading too many newspapers."

"Maybe," she shrugged, focusing down at the typewriter, just as if she couldn't feed the paper in by sheer muscle-memory. "I mean... I don't know..." she started after a beat, her eyes shifting back up to search him. "What do you think, Horus? Do you think it's possible there's a smidgeon of truth to any of the wild things they say can happen during a Syzygy?"

"I seriously doubt it," he replied. He searched her back, raising a brow. "You're not the least worried about it, are you?"

"Me? No... of course not. I was just curious what *you* thought of it."

"Very little, honestly," he admitted. "I anchor myself with the knowledge that the universe the Creators fashioned is subject to carefully balanced forces, predictable in their ebb and flow. There's no reason to be troubled by superstition." He grinned an encouraging grin. "Wouldn't you agree?"

"Oh yes," she nodded emphatically. "Certainly."

"I'm glad," he said... sensing a chance to fish for information... looking away coyly. "Because, you know, if something really *was* bothering you, I hope you'd tell me. I hope you would know that I'm always here to help."

She looked at him dumbfounded. "What... what makes you say that?"

He shook his head. "Nothing, perhaps. Maybe my own imagination is just running away with prevailing trends. I've been subjected to a lot of heavy secrets lately... even as I search for yet others. But you know, it's a funny thing: I think in every case, the truth would've been a simple remedy. After all, being upfront is always the best policy."

Suddenly, there was a knock at the door. They both froze, exchanging a look that read, *'He noticed'*. There was another knock. Horus sighed a *'so-much-for-getting-any-work-done'* sigh, and went for the door. As he opened it, though, he quickly discovered: It *wasn't* Eb Thalymus. Far from it. But he could hardly believe who it *was*...

"Good evening, Counselor Templar," Dr. Nokkaeru greeted him. "I hope you don't mind my stopping in to cordially remind you: I know where you live, and am thus liable to appear at *any* time. Is your secretary present, perchance?"

Horus abruptly shut the door.

"That didn't sound at all like Eb," Deborah remarked.

"It wasn't," he answered breathlessly.

"Well then who...?" she began, but was abruptly cut off by a third knock at the door. Only this time, it was the *other* door...

Again, they remained stunned, until whomever was outside rapped on the car still one more time. "That really *did* come from the other door..." Deborah marveled.

"So it seems," Horus was obliged to say.

"Whoever's out there must be speedy," she went on, shaking her head and turning to answer. "I'll get it this time..."

"Wait... you shouldn't..." Horus stammered. But it was too late...

"Hiya, Debs," Art said, filling the back threshold. "What's shakin'? I've got an update for ya. It's about... well... you know." He winked.

Deborah abruptly shut the back door.

"...That was Art, wasn't it?" Horus asked at length.

"Yes," Deborah laughed nervously. "The big lug himself. Was he the one at your door?"

"Why no," Horus answered.

There was a moment of silence.

"Well then... who was it?"

Horus looked around, grasping at plausible explanations for the answer. "Uh, well... oddly enough... it was..."

The front door burst open.

"That was not so courteous, Counselor," Nokkaeru grumbled. "But no matter; I have done what your manners failed to do and let myself in. I don't suppose you would care to rectify your gaffe and offer a lady a perch? Or, do you mean to go on being impolite without cause?"

"Dr. Nokkaeru?" Deborah asked, incredulous. "Why, whatever brings you here?"

"Ah, *Deborah Boulevard*..." Nokkaeru intoned, her voice a low and sinister music. "What a truly expedient question for you to venture. Gladly, I will tell you in exhaustive detail..."

Just before Horus could implode, the door behind Deborah opened, and all took note...

"What was that about?" Art asked, looking down at Deborah as he waltzed on in. "You almost busted my nose."

She turned her palms up, grinning toothily. "Sorry, Art... didn't see you there."

Art eyed her doubtfully. "Yer acting real funny, Debs." He leaned in cautiously, holding up a hand as he went on in discreet tones. "*Do you think you're having more symptoms*?"

"How very interesting," Nokkaeru interjected, angling at Horus. "Your friend the investigator seems to be attempting to carry on some sort of private conversation with your secretary. How does that make you feel, Counselor? Does it incite you to envy? I am *sure* you will remember learning: I am versed in psychiatric care, now."

"I remember... however incidentally," Horus said, tugging at his collar. "I can only imagine all the training that must've entailed. About neuroses... psychopharmacology... *patient confidentiality...*"

"What's the bird doctor doing here?" Art asked Deborah. "Did you go and get your own second opinion?"

"Second opinion?" Horus asked.

Deborah shrugged. "Oh, I might've told Art about my little head-cold," she explained. "I'm ***sure*** that's all he means..."

"Yup, she's right!" Art went along, nodding endlessly as he picked up on her *suggestion*. "It's definitely that and nothing else."

"But I seem to have come at just the right moment!" Nokkaeru exclaimed. "Ms. Boulevard, I urge you: Do not let even a mild sickness go undiagnosed. Seek an appointment. Do it for yourself. What is more: do it for your *employer*. You have no idea the toll it would take on him, if you were to succumb suddenly to grave illness."

"Now wait just a minute," Art put in, stepping forward.

"Art, please, just..." Deborah tried.

"It's alright, Debs, I got this," Art insisted, before pointing accusingly at the Doctor. "Listen here: She doesn't need any appointment because there is absolutely nothing weird going on with her at all, and that's final."

"Art," Deborah fumed, *"zip it."*

Nokkaeru tsked. "Do you see the way Detective Mallard comes to her defense? Such brash, ignorant chivalry. I fear you may indeed have a rival in him, Counselor."

"'Rival?'" Deborah asked. "What are you talking about?" She shot Horus a questioning look. "Horus, do you know what she's doing here?"

"I'm sure I don't!" he appealed, turning to Nokkaeru. "Really, Doctor: I'm as helpless as anyone to decipher a word of what you've said so far. Moreover, while I *do* regret to be rude, the fact remains you've caught Deborah and I in the middle of some important business. Now, if you have anything coherent to share, perhaps I can visit you in your *own* office some other time, at your convenience. But whatever it is, I'm afraid I must insist that this is neither the time nor the place for it."

The Doctor fluttered, after which they could hear her neck feathers curl up under their leather sleeve. *"Incoherent,* am I? I make that a very poor choice of words, Horus Templar. For, until this moment, I had only a mind to frazzle you with vague suggestions – to amuse myself with a few fleeting minutes of your anxiety, before leaving you quite without permanent damage. But you have indeed been *rude*. And now, I think, I am inclined to make you pay for it. So, let me see if I can articulate this in a way that is *coherent* enough for your liking. You... Horus son of Tanis... have long harbored..."

...She was suddenly cut off, when once again, there was loud thumping at the door. "What in tarnation is a'goin' on in there!? I heard raised voices! Is y' in a fix?! I'll come in scrappin' at yer say-so!"

Horus was overwhelmed at once with a rushing wind of hope – elated at the very voice he'd come so much to dread. "Eb! How timely of you! It's alright; we're not in any trouble. Actually, you're missing out on quite a merry gathering. Won't you come in and meet our friends?"

At Horus' invitation, Eb let himself heroically into the car. "Some to-do you fellers is a-puttin' on. I coulda swored somebody was gittin' their whiskers pulled off over here! But now, who's y' friends? I'll be pleased ta make their acquaintance."

"Who are *we*?" Nokkaeru demanded impatiently. "The question, Sir, is who are *you*?"

"I'm so glad you asked," Horus put in. "Nokkaeru, this is Nebuchadnezzar Thalymus. Eb, meet Doctor Nokkaeru."

"Nokkaeru... an honest-ta-goodness Plague Doctor!" He knelt down to take and lick her talon. "It's an honor, ma'am."

"Thank you," she replied meekly, despite herself... after which, she shook herself, rekindling her venom. "But really, of all the *wily*...!"

"...And this is Artimus Mallard, Private Detective," Deborah went along, bodily pushing Art to the forefront. "He's been eager to meet you for some time now."

"That's right!" Horus went along, perhaps a bit too enthusiastically. He quickly cleared his throat. "In fact, they both have."

"*I most certainly have n...!*" the Doctor tried, but to no avail.

"...Why shucks!" Eb declared. "Imagine a fancy doctor lady an' the *famous* Art Mallard comin' to call on little ol' me!"

"Gadzooks!" Art replied. "You mean, you've heard of me, too? That's really neat."

Eb reached out and shook Art's hand. "Well, 'course I have! Yer mentor was a friend o' mine... an old, old friend. We worked some *fine* cases t'gether!"

"It's wonderful to see you all getting on so well," Horus remarked. "Eb, would you do us a great service and entertain our guests for a while?

Deborah and I have something to type up, after which we're free to join you. If it's not too much trouble, that is."

"Trouble!?" he asked, aghast. "Why Horus, I'd like nothin' better!"

"Inconceivable!" Nokkaeru interjected. "I decline! I stalwartly refuse to be foisted on..."

"Naw, Naw, Doctor," Eb reassured her, even as he corralled her and Art, leading them to the doorway. "Ya got no cause ta fret. Jist 'cause I got some history with this here young feller's old forerunner don't mean you's gonna be left out! I'll make good'n sure o' that! Why, I's had all kind o' sickness an' infirmity in ma life thet we can talk about! You know much about dentistry? Mercy, but I've had some cantankerous chompers! Naw take this one molar I've got here way in the back..."

Horus and Deborah formed a united front and closed the door behind the three of them, heaving a breath of relief so deep that it was exhausting in its own right. As they recovered, Deborah eventually looked up into Horus' eyes. "Horus..." she said. "Let's..."

"...Forget everything that just happened and get back to work?" he put in.

She nodded with a grin. "My thoughts exactly."

* * *

Shortly after sitting down a second time to type Horus' speech endorsing the prisoner exchange, the train began its first nightly circuit. They had time to finish the whole stirring call to 'honor and patriotism and whatnot', and still there was a good deal of track ahead of them. After all the evening had brought them, they weren't greatly troubled to rest a while in peace and quiet. But, as the circuit ended, their conscience prevailed, and they were moved with compassion for those they'd left to a dismal fate...

"Well, we've spent the evening calling for the redemption of prisoners," Deborah remarked at length. "Would we be terribly hypocritical now if we didn't try and rescue Art and the Doctor from Eb?"

"I'm afraid we would," Horus answered.

Having established that much, they neither moved nor stirred for several seconds.

Finally, Horus drew himself up with a groan, feeling utterly exhausted. "Why don't I take the fall, and you can head home for the night? Get some sleep?"

She sprang up suddenly. "I can do it, if you'd rather..."

He waved her down. "No, it's alright. I'd just as soon take care of it. The Doctor seemed to be in an ugly mood... and that was *before* we sent her away with Eb."

She made a face. "Do you think you could send Art in here, before he goes? I never did find him back at Civil Headquarters."

He huffed tiredly. *"Again* with Art. Why has he suddenly become so...?" He stopped himself, shocked by his own words.

Deborah said nothing... she only looked on.

"Well, never mind," he said, hanging his head. "Of course, I can't promise anything. We might all three be caught in Eb's web. But I'll see what I can do."

"Thanks, Boss."

He nodded, then slowly ventured out of the car...

Trudging into the dark, Horus found he had to make a point of mustering himself. He took a deep breath, drew himself up, crossed the coupling, and then – lingering outside the door to Eb's car only a few seconds longer – reached for the nob...

But to his amazement, the door came open on its own. Staring with unbelief, he lost a moment before stepping out of the way of a thoroughly shell-shocked-looking Art and Nokkaeru, shuffling out onto the veranda...

"Wow," Art summed it up, staring off many thousands of yards. "That guy can *talk*. Like, the stuff he said was kinda interesting for a while. But then it just kept coming. And *coming*. I didn't want to listen anymore... but somehow, I *had* to. There was no other choice. It was the darndest thing..."

"You describe it well, Detective Mallard," Nokkaeru agreed, sounding every bit as diminished as he did. "There was... a *compulsion*... in the way he slowly expounded each meaningless anecdote. Even one such as I – who has no regard whatever for the feelings of others – was helpless against it... a paralytic hostage of his endless word-sludge." She shook her head, beleaguered. "Such a phenomenon. I have never seen its like, and I hope never to again."

"Heh," Art laughed. "Now you know about what it's like to be hypnotized."

"But I don't understand," Horus interjected. "How did the two of you escape?" He could form only one, rather unpleasant conclusion. "Did you sedate him, Doctor?"

"Would that I had thought of it, but no. Fortunately, his advanced age proved sedative enough, with scarcely a bend or two left in the track before we pulled into the station. He suddenly nodded off right in the middle of a raucous description of his bunions."

"Ironic, isn't it?" Art mused. "The same seniority that made him so mesmerizing to listen to is what saved us in the end."

"Poetic indeed," Nokkaeru nodded.

"Well, I meant to come out and save you myself, if I could," Horus lamented. "But I suppose there's no use crowing it now. I've come too late to make any recompense for what I put you through."

"And yet, just the same, the gale has passed," the Doctor replied, "and it is hard not to see the world in a more forgiving light. I recognize the courage it took, just to bring you to this door, knowing the onslaught that should've awaited you beyond. And I am... *grateful*... though the very word pains me to speak aloud."

"Yeah, thanks Buddy," Art concurred. Presently he shot a look at his watch, whistling. "I've gotta get going... I have a date tonight."

"Yes, of course," Horus replied, reluctantly remembering what Deborah had asked. "Would you stop in and see Deborah first? She seems to have something more she wanted to talk to you about."

"Oh... right," Art said. "There was still that one very uninteresting thing I didn't get to tell her. Thanks for reminding me. See ya, Horus... Nokkaeru."

"May the Creators speed your journey, friend Mallard," Nokkaeru replied.

Horus blinked. "See you later, Art," he said finally. But after Art had disappeared into his office, he turned his bewildered look on Nokkaeru. "That was rather a kind word from you, Doctor. I would never have guessed you esteem Art so highly."

"We are comrades now in great hardship," she explained. Then, she turned to face Horus. "As for you, Counselor Templar: What shall I do with you? You have insulted, outmaneuvered and utterly exasperated me this night. I should hate you for it. I should make good on my threats to expose your secret. You know there is nothing stopping me."

"Isn't there?" Horus challenged, forced to grasp at straws. "You work awfully hard to come across as a cruel, uncaring person, Doctor. I wonder why."

"It is no effort... nor any act. Would you go out of your way to avoid bending a blade of grass, Counselor? I think not. We all tread without thought on what we deem superfluous. If my stride is a bit heavier – a bit more deliberate – then perhaps I walk a little higher than most. And I deem few things so superfluous as *feelings*... romance in especial."

"That's interesting," said Horus. "It seems to me I've heard the ones who most disdain love are the ones who've been scarred the deepest by it."

Her goggles silently reflected Other-Worldly light, then turned away. "Do not presume to know a thing about me," she quietly instructed him. "You can be sure you will gain nothing that way."

He shrugged. "Well, I guess we all have our secrets. You reminded me dramatically enough of that today. But of course, you're right: I can only speculate what *yours* are. On the other hand, you *know* mine... and there's no way I can stop you from doing whatever you will with it. I'm at your mercy."

"That is a most dreadful place for you to be," she boded.

"Yes. Believe me, I know."

They fell silent again. The quiet steadily grew until it was tense. Then finally, Nokkaeru broke it...

"Your secret will remain a while with me, Counselor," she grudged. "Not as any favor or courtesy, mind you. But it occurs: If I were to expose you, what then would I savor getting to hold over your head?"

Horus chuckled. "Well, there's always your old bit about my future calamity."

"True," she granted. "But its long delay begins to wear on my patience. This is the only thing I have to tide me over. Perhaps it would be shortsighted on my part to waste it."

"That's a theory I can get behind," he said. "But I hope you won't make a habit of these house calls."

She shook her head. "Having a bit of levity at your expense was only the business I led with. There is something more I have yet to relay."

Horus' ears perked. "Really? That is, I would never have guessed."

"You take much for granted, Counselor. Why do you think I was so wroth, being put off? You simply *assumed* I had only come to torture you."

"Well let's have it! We're overdue for a step forward on the Tweed case!"

"Then prepare yourself for a disappointment, because this will be more like a step back," she warned, stealing to the back of the veranda. "But to best convey my discovery, I think we must have a demonstration. Come, Counselor Templar. You must simulate my strangulation."

He blinked. "I... *what*?"

"Oh, don't belabor this with your civility," she said tiredly. "We are recreating the crime, as I had pictured it. I assure you it is important. There is no danger. Now do as I say, so that you may learn something."

He shook his head, but reluctantly agreed. "I did find myself wishing for a way to shut you up before, but never like this." He cupped his hands loosely in front of her throat. "Is this right?"

"Do you really need to be instructed how to strangle someone?" she asked sarcastically. "You are about the throat, and that is what counts... if you didn't know. But you will have to actually hold on, so I do not lose my balance for my part of the simulation."

"I don't like this at all," he wavered. "How long before I let go? What if I hurt you?"

"Blast it, Counselor, just do it, and this will all be over before you can fully form another second thought!"

"Alright..." he sighed. Aversely, he pushed his hands around the leather sleeve of her neck... surely, the most awkward thing he'd ever done. Within a moment, he was just about to let go and condemn the whole experiment when she quickly shifted, and his entire forearm erupted in burning, shooting pain. At this point, he dropped her anyway, reflexively cradling his injury...

"There, was that really so hard?" she asked.

"In more ways than I guessed," he replied, forcing each word through clenched teeth while his eyes starred-up. "That was some uppercut. It feels like you broke my arm."

"Ah, but what *part* of your arm?"

"The bottom... right where you struck it, of course," he said, still waiting for some relief. "This is definitely going to bruise."

"Exactly," she framed it. "In much the same place that Tweed's arms were bruised."

Horus' clenched eyes opened. He regarded her. "You... you struck the bottom of my arm... because you had to punch with your *leg*..."

She nodded. "You see then what I'm driving at, Counselor. When I told you his injuries were consistent with the defensive wounds of strangulation, I neglected to adequately consider some of the physical realities. I knew that if *I* were strangled, I would punch upward with my legs. But in the case of an anthropomorphic victim..."

"...The bruising would be on the *top* of the arm. We would use our own arms to try to beat his *down*."

"Precisely."

He began to stroke his chin. "So then... what is your verdict *now*?"

"There are two main possibilities," she explained. "Either Tweed's mystery victim was a Heron... which I make very unlikely. Or, the bruises I found may have no forensic bearing on the investigation at all. They have merely been red herrings all along."

Horus sighed. "That really *does* feel like a step back. But... it's closer to the truth. And the truth is never in the wrong direction."

"Well, you've learned what I had to teach you," Nokkaeru said, making her way down the steps. "And, if we've progressed to adages, then I suppose I'll be going."

"You have my thanks, Doctor," he called after her. "For the school of hard knocks... and for your discretion, too."

She stopped, half-turning her head back to speak. "You know, Horus Templar, I've no idea what is to be done about Tweed. But as for your other problem, there *is* a solution, which you seem to have neglected."

"What's that?" he asked, earnestly oblivious.

"You could simply talk to Ms. Boulevard yourself. In that instance, I would be powerless."

Horus suppressed a laugh, marveling at her words. The solution was indeed simple, as it was impossible. And suddenly, he was obliged to regurgitate the same lame answer he'd been hearing so often himself...

"I'll think about it."

* * *

"I don't know how much more of this I can take," Deborah sighed, pacing the floor. "Why couldn't you have just been at Headquarters earlier when I had a chance to find you on my own?"

Art sat back, quietly drumming on the arm of his chair. "Well, the fact of the matter is, I *was* there... but it's no wonder you couldn't find me. I got tied up a long time in Requisitions."

"*Requisitions*? Why would you be...?" She stopped herself. "It doesn't matter. We're here now... what did you learn today?"

"I'm honestly not sure," Art admitted.

Her look wasn't friendly. "Are you kidding me? You said you had an update! Didn't you see a Thinker?"

"Sure did."

"Well, how could you come away from that and not know what you learned?"

Art shrugged. "It's just his way. You would've had to be there. He told me Werehumans are definitely real. But he also told me half of what he says is fake."

"So basically we're back to square one," she said, brushing a hand across her neck. "But you know what this means: You're stuck watching my house tonight."

"Yup," he said, unphased.

She waited suspiciously. "And you're... okay with that? What about your date with Blucille?"

"Not a problem." He stood up, tugging on his jacket smugly. "You underestimate my resourcefulness, Debs. I got it all worked out. Go on home, get some rest, and don't worry about a thing. I'm just clever enough to kill two birds with one stone."

Chapter 12

"So this is what you meant by mixing business with pleasure," Blucille said, adjusting her binoculars as they sat in a police carriage, parked inconspicuously across the street from a quiet little house. "I'm not sure whether I'm disappointed or just confused."

"Stakeouts aren't your favorite, huh?" Art replied, running another slow sweep of the yard through his own field glasses. "I'll keep that in mind for next time."

"Well, I couldn't really say if they're my 'favorite' or not. Stakeouts aren't exactly in the scope of a District Attorney's duties."

"Well there ya go, then!" he exclaimed, taking a moment to look back and give her an encouraging grin. "Something exciting and new for ya."

"*New*, anyway," she sighed, though she went on diligently scanning. "It might help matters slightly if you could tell me what we're supposed to be looking for."

"Sorry... no can do," Art said. "That's privileged information."

A few seconds of quiet observation passed. And then, just when Art began to think he was in the clear, Blucille asked, "Isn't this Deborah Boulevard's house?"

He was inclined to panic, but managed to stay very cool. "Is it really? Heh, whatdaya know about that."

He could feel her eyes on him...

"Some romantic you are... inviting me along for an evening of watching another woman's house," she quipped.

"Hey, now," he began defensively. "Don't go making Debs into 'another woman' all of a sudden. She and I are just pals, you know that."

"Oh, I know," she relented with a groan. "And I really didn't think myself the jealous or suspicious type. It's never bothered me before. But..."

He turned to her, looking concerned. "But what?"

"Well, things have just been a little strange lately."

"*Strange*?" he chuckled. "I can't imagine what you mean."

"Okay then... I'll spell it out. First, you start inventing these clunky excuses to go talk with her..."

"Clunky?" he interjected, honestly surprised.

"...Now, you cancel our plans last-minute, apparently so we can spend the night spying on her property without any explanation."

"I guess that would seem a little unusual, but..."

"...And what's more, you brought Captain Alexei along," she went on, gesturing to the front of the carriage.

"*Me*?" Alexei protested, setting down his own binoculars. "You are going to take exception with *me* now? I rather like to think I've been a most unobtrusive chaperone in this endeavor. Why must *I* be corralled into the spat?"

"Maybe because I have no idea *why* you're a part of this endeavor at all," Blucille explained as she shifted her look back to Art.

"Well, this *is* a police stakeout, isn't it?" Art contended. "I just figured we needed a policeman with us, in case we have to make a formal arrest."

"And I daresay it's just as well I'm here," Alexei shrugged. "I decline to explain why, but suffice it to say, the less I am around the house to answer questions, the better. It is actually quite fortuitous that you invited me along, out of all the prospective badges at your disposal."

Blucille shot him a look. "Would you mind going back into 'unobtrusive' mode, *Captain*?"

Alexei snickered nervously. "Sorry, Ma'am. Don't mind me." He picked the binoculars back up.

Blucille turned back to her date. "Art... *why* in the world would we have to make an arrest? I mean really... this is starting to get serious. Maybe up to this point I've just been nosey, but now we're talking about civic order. I think you're obligated to tell us what's *really* going on."

He eyed her pleadingly. He didn't want to cave, but already it felt like all he could do. "You gotta promise not to repeat anything I tell you. It's kind of a big secret."

She sighed. "Alright."

Art turned to Alexei. "That goes for you too, Sirens."

He held up a hand solemnly. "I resolve to disclose nothing except that which might inevitably need to be reported in connection with any arrest... or that my wife drags out of me."

Art shrugged. "I guess that'll have to be good enough." His eyes danced between each of them. "Debs thinks she's turning into a Werehuman at night."

Blucille went blank. Then, at great length, her eyes narrowed. "Nice try."

"No really! I mean it!" Art insisted. "What with the Syzygy and her great-grandfather and the bald patches on her elbows and stuff, she's really cut up! And I've *tried* to prove it's all superstition, but even after all this time I haven't been able to do it. So this is kind of our last resort... watching over her while she sleeps and seeing if anything comes of it."

Blucille looked very much unmoved. But she deferred to Alexei. "What do you think, Captain?"

"I believe him, Ms. Cordon," he answered. "This does not even rank with the strangest stories I've heard in the last few days."

She returned to searching Art's eyes, softening after only a moment. "Okay. I guess if I got some crazy idea that I was transforming into a terror in my sleep, I'd be looking for the same kind of help... and the same confidentiality. I *am* sorry to pry, Art. I should've known you were just being a good friend, in your own strange way."

He grinned. "Don't sweat it, Tulip Toes. Honestly, it's better that you know. Now you can be way more help keeping watch!"

"Right..." she reluctantly assented, pointing her snout out the window. "I guess it's back to our fun-filled evening."

"Ah, come on, Blucille," Art encouraged her. "We can still make this a proper date. Think about it: We have all kinds of quiet time to get to know each other." He gestured at himself. "Go on, ask me something. Anything you've been dying to know."

She did seem to perk up at the offer. "Okay, well, I've been sort of curious what your childhood was like," she admitted, shifting in her seat. "What can you tell me about the young Art Mallard? Were there signs right from the start that you could grow up to be a great detective?"

"Ha!" he exclaimed. "Not hardly. Actually, if you'll believe it, my folks thought I was kinda dense."

"I can't imagine," she said, shaking her head. "Well, did you show an affinity for anything else? Did you have any special talents?"

"Heh, only one I can distinctly remember. But it's kinda embarrassing."

"Go on," she verbally nudged him. "Tell me anyway. I won't judge."

"Well..." he started, "...I was pretty good at burping the A-B-C's."

"*Get out of town*," she breathed blankly.

Art grinned nervously. "Yeah, see, I figured you'd think it was stupid."

"No!" she protested. "It's not that at all! It's just... well... I used to do the same thing!"

He could hardly contain his sudden joy. "No foolin'?! Wow, that's far out!" He waved giddily in his own direction. "You gotta tell me: What letter was your favorite? Mine was definitely 'B'!"

"That's amazing!" she replied. "So was mine!"

"Unreal! But then, why should I be surprised? 'B' was always special. There was just something so full-bodied about the way it could be belched, don't ya think?"

"Exactly!" she laughed.

"*Augh*, it's been so long!" he thought aloud. "I wonder if I still got it..." He sucked in a breath, then he gave it his best shot. "*BEEEEEEEE*"

"Not bad," Blucille nodded. "...For a beginner, anyway."

"*Oh*?" he asked playfully. "I suppose you can do better?"

He watched her situate herself, like she had a whole refined technique to it...

"*BEEEE*"

"Wowser," Art remarked. "That *was* pretty good! A little brief, though."

"For me, it was always more about sonic quality than duration. But I've got a longer one if you want it. I'm just getting warmed up."

"Me too!"

And so, the duel began...

"*BEEEEEEEE*"

"*BEEEEEEEEEE*"

"*BEEEEEE*"

"Creators above!" Alexei finally burst. "I fear for the healthy development of my marriage, if this is what growing in emotional intimacy looks like! You are making a *scene*!"

Art and Blucille exchanged a look, each donning apologetic smiles. "Sorry, Mac," Art offered on their behalf. "Kinda forgot you were there."

Alexei sighed. "So I had intended... yet you've pushed me beyond the limits of my tolerance. Even so, I am sorry to hamper your enthusiasm. Perhaps I could step out for a moment. I am sure the horses could use tending..."

"We could go on a walkabout ourselves," Blucille suggested, looking at Art. "Surely Alexei could handle the stakeout on his own for a while, now that he knows what to look for."

Art turned his eyes to Alexei. "How 'bout it, Chaperone? Think you could handle the business side of things for a bit?"

He nodded rather energetically. "By all means! The two of you may take your time."

Art looked back at Blucille. "You heard the fella. Let's go for a walk."

* * *

They spent a while simply walking around the block in silence, trying to savor the sights and sounds of the suburbs. But what began with obvious aspirations of being an idyllic little stroll quickly became, well, sort of awkward. It started early, when, after leaving their *own* inconspicuous fully-hitched carriage, they noticed a similar one parked just a couple spaces behind them. Needless to say, it was an uncommon sight for the middle of the night, and the watchers were forced to wonder if they themselves were being watched...

It wasn't until they rounded the first corner that they really managed to shrug the mystery of the second carriage off. They came upon a hedge of lilac bushes, and Blucille paused to enjoy the fragrance of the flowers. Not really caring for lilacs any more than Blucille cared for lavender, Art rather absently propped himself up on the nearest impediment in the sidewalk, striking a cool pose while she sniffed, just the way that any true fashion plate would do. However, this led to its own gaffe, when she looked back at him – appearing confused and rather disgusted – and he discovered much too late that what he assumed was just a half-finished lamppost was actually a *fire hydrant*! He simply couldn't fling himself away fast enough to avoid grave embarrassment. Hydrants, after all, were such vexingly crude-looking structures... like whoever designed them had done everything in their power to evoke a mighty urge to go to the bathroom. Art could only grin sheepishly as they slowly began to walk away from the scene...

Hardly had the humiliation began to subside, and Blucille made something of a tactical error in trying to pivot to small-talk. "It's bright out tonight," she commented.

"Yeah..." Art agreed. They both took stunted looks directly up at the Other Worlds before abruptly casting their eyes back down. Of course, for all either of them knew, the Syzygy might still be complete bunk... but under the double-light of a nearly perfect row of planets, the uncertainty proved a bit uncomfortable...

"How 'bout those crickets?" Art tried, noticing their droning for the first time in the uneasy quiet. "You don't get *that* in the city proper."

"Crickets?" Blucille repeated. "I don't know what that noise is, but it's not like any crickets I ever heard."

Art puzzled a moment. "Well, if it's not crickets... what else would be buzzing on and on like that?"

She was not quick with an answer. "I don't know," she finally admitted.

They continued on, more uncomfortable than ever...

With only one corner left to go before they returned to the carriage, Art made a final attempt to salvage the occasion. He noted a park bench under a streetlamp just beside the path with a favorable view of some big old trees. He motioned for them to have a seat, and Blucille silently but readily obliged. The two of them huddled close, looking out...

"This is nice," she claimed, after a while.

Art chuckled. "Nice, eh? That's a polite way of putting it."

"Okay, so it's been a little weird," she replied, throwing her hands up dismissively. "What else is new?"

They laughed.

"Ya know, I honestly thought that disgusting fire hydrant was just a lamppost," he threw in, while the mood was still easy.

"It was pretty comical to watch you leap like that," she went on laughing. "I might've split a gut right there, if I wasn't trying so hard not to sneeze. Those flowers smelled like burnt sea-cucumbers!"

Art's own laughter wound-down awkwardly from there, back into silence. Once again, they'd come to a roadblock...

"Art..." Blucille began again, low and reserved. "You... you said earlier that I could ask you anything. Was that just the excitement of the moment talking? That is, did you really mean it?"

"Sure I did," Art replied, donning a confident expression. "You got something else? Let's hear it! Beats listening to the non-crickets."

She looked away. "Well, if you didn't think I was the jealous type before, I guess I'm about to seal it."

He shrugged. "A question's a question. Go ahead... what's on your mind?"

She turned back, searching him. "Was there ever anyone else in your life, Art? Anyone else that was really special to you?" She threw a hand out as she blanched. "I mean, I don't mean to suggest *I'm* all that special or anything... but..." she trailed off, looking frantic and embarrassed.

"There was never anyone else," he answered simply. "Oh, don't get me wrong: I've been out with a few classy dames before. But when it didn't work out, I guess I was never cut up for too long."

She sighed, letting her hat hide her head. "I'm sorry... it was a stupid question. You were kind to even answer it."

"No problem, Toots," Art assured her. "It doesn't bother me. If anything, I'm just a little surprised you'd ask."

"Oh?" she wondered aloud. "Why's that?"

Art felt a catch in his throat. Always, he seemed to be speaking his mind a little too freely. "You're gonna make me put *my* foot in my mouth now," he said, trying to come up with a delicate but honest answer. "It just seems like... if you asked me about my romantic history... well... I might've bumbled right along and asked about *yours*... before I had a chance to think better of it. But I gather that's something you'd rather not talk about. And that's fine! If it's easier for you to deal with the past privately, I'll just have to trust that you would know better than I would. I'm not about to drag it out of ya."

As he spoke, she appeared astonished. Her gaze fell. Art panicked...

"No, wait!" he appealed. "I can see how that might sound insincere, but it's the truth!! Please don't take me for a snoop again! I'll ask you something else! I have a million other questions! What's your favorite color?"

"We grew up together, he and I," she replied softly. Her eyes returned to the level, gazing off into nothing. "It's funny the way I can remember some of the earliest times the best. We used to love to pick dirt clogs out of the street between our houses and crush them in our hands. I helped him learn how to tie his shoes, and he used to spit on my head and smooth out this one wild curl in my fur. And that was all before we even exchanged names..." She looked to Art. "Let me tell you, *that* really turned into something. I remember... we were so amazed when we found out that both our names started with a 'B'. To a couple little kids, it was a profound moment of destiny. But then... it wound up taking quite a turn for the worse, for a while there..."

"Oh?" Art inquired without a thought, too spellbound by this glimpse into a powerful, formative memory to even consider how small he felt next to it.

She nodded. "He came up to me soon after and announced that, 'Lucille starts with "L".' He was convinced I'd lied to him. We didn't speak for weeks." She paused on this point for a while. "That was the biggest fight we ever had." Art watched her eyes dance as she sifted through the years, perhaps trying to hold back tears in the same action. "I wonder now... if all his ridiculous pet-names for me grew out of that ordeal. I didn't mind them... not for long, anyway. He could call me whatever he liked. But I always called him by his name." She focused questioningly on Art. "Because it was *him*, you know? All that he was, in one special little word."

"What *was* his name?" Art asked… another reflex. He waved a hand. "I mean, if it's not too much to ask!"

She only grinned shyly. "His name… his name was Bob."

Quite suddenly, Art had to call on all his willpower not to laugh. "Bob?" he repeated despite himself. "The special little word was Bob?"

"Oh, I know how silly that sounds, believe me," she replied, fortunately not hurt. "It's probably the most no-frills name anyone ever came up with. But, I don't know… I can't say exactly where or when it happened, but I got to the point where just the sound of it had a sort of music. Saying his name was like singing a little song. A song that captured so many of life's best moments… and dearest hopes…" Art saw her eyes finally moisten, just before she turned away again. "I'm sorry. This isn't something I really talk about. I thought… maybe now I could. But wouldn't you know? Turns out it's still hard."

This proved a lot for Art to process. His own emotions ran high, even as they tried to pull him in a dozen different directions. Should he be hurt? Or humiliated? Who was he, compared with this 'Bob'… whose very name she cherished? How much more was there to know? And what had ultimately happened to leave her like this – alone and heartbroken? Was it something Bob did? Was it something *Blucille* had done? Art never meant to unseal the matter in the first place… but how could he let her stop now?

But while he was still mired deep in thought, she went on to mutter a final conclusion…

"I've taken to wishing I could simply forget."

Art shook away all his questions; they were selfish. Seeing her in her misery, it wasn't hard to find the strength to respond as he should. He set a hand on her shoulder…

"I'm the one who's sorry, Blucille. I can't imagine what you've been through. But I know what it's like to have some of your most precious memories turned against you. And I can tell you: forgetting is no comfort. You're only left to wonder what you've lost."

She sniffled. "You… you haven't completely recovered from your time with the Digit Cults, have you?"

"Not if I'm honest."

She took the hand he'd placed on her shoulder in between her own, regarding him with serious but kind eyes. "Tell me about it. Tell me about what you're going through."

He shrugged. "Well, I don't know, exactly," he chuckled half-heartedly, gesturing to his head. "I might still have everything important stored up here somewhere. Then again, I might not. There's probably no way I'll ever know for sure."

"That's awful," was all she could say.

"It *has* gotten better," Art assured her. "I'm not gonna lie: The first few weeks were rough. Life was such a haze; I could never be sure I wasn't stuck in another one of Sabracore's illusions. Sometimes... sometimes I really worried I was. Especially nights... quiet, closed-in nights when I'd struggle to fall asleep. I was always so afraid I'd wake back up in the cell..." He managed a grin. "But I feel more sure now. And I sleep a lot better."

She grinned back. "You must have some real strength hidden behind all that muscle, Art. I'm sure I would've cracked in your place."

"Well that's almost funny," he said.

"What is?"

It was his turn to look away, embarrassed. "You... you *were* some of my strength, in the thick of it. I mean, it's all still a blur... I can't be sure about much of anything that happened in that old warehouse. They were doing their darndest to make me forget everyone... and everything. I fought tooth and nail for every memory I had. But I honestly think I tried harder to remember you than anyone."

There was a glimmer in her eyes, just then... a flicker of a kind of amazement that Art was quite certain he'd never had directed at him before. He was more than a little amazed himself. Here, he'd just spilled his guts... he'd admitted something rather profound, and compromising. But she wasn't humiliated... or revolted. She was joyful. And having her sitting there with him, in the wash of light from a strand of crazy Worlds, holding his hand and looking into his eyes with such joy, he could only think how much he wanted to lean in and gently lick the side of her face...

...Carried on the wings of a thousand butterflies, he slowly craned his snout in her direction...

...She made no sign to deter him...

BRRRRRRRRRRRRRRRdrrrrRRRRdrrRR!

Art and Blucille both froze wide-eyed as a police whistle split the air. They just looked at each other – horrified – until Alexei blared a second call. The moment was lost. They leapt into action...

Rounding the last corner in the block, they had only enough time to recognize the wiry frame of the police captain before he overtook and leapt on another figure in the darkness. They went bounding up to him, struggling to catch a clear glimpse of the creature Alexei was now grappling on the ground...

"Ms. Boulevard!" Alexei called out. "Ms. Boulevard, stop! It is I, Captain Alexei! You must desist! We are only here to help you!"

"No!" a woman's voice replied. "No, let me go! I'm not the one you want! I've done nothing wrong!"

"I don't believe it," Art marveled, now standing over the struggle. "It's *true*. She's actually turning into a Werehuman... and we caught her in the act..."

Blucille's face contorted. "I'm... not so sure..."

She leaned down, helping the Captain wrestle his assailant over, where her face could be seen. And after a moment, they had eyes on her: a terrified-looking Human... or what could certainly pass for one...

"Deborah Boulevard, please!" Alexei implored her. "You must cease! I am sorry, but you cannot be permitted free range in your present condition. You are a liability to this city!"

"I don't know what you're talking about!" the creature insisted. "Who is Deborah Boulevard?! My name is Hailey Barborough!"

Art, Blucille, and Alexei blanched. They turned a look back over their shoulders, just in time to watch that mysterious second carriage begin to pull away...

They returned to Alexei...

"Captain..." Blucille began. "Did you actually *see* this woman come out of Deborah's house?"

"I..." he stammered. "She... she came round from the back. But surely she had no cause to pass it by so close, unless she..."

"Did you ***see*** her come out of the house?"

He looked back at them, even as he kept a hold on the woman's arms. "No. No I didn't."

For a while, the four of them could only exchange dumbfounded, mortified expressions. Alexei, Art, Blucille... and *Hailey Barborough*...

Chapter 13

It was a morning of fateful snippets. Everywhere Horus turned, the people were rushing around at double-speed, or else huddling into little murmuring groups. The smells and sights of fear were enough to cause him a moment of anxiety. However, he quickly remembered learning that superstitions about the Syzygy were popularly felt, and that the news had lately been preying on those misgivings. With the Syzygy now nearing its apex, an escalation of tension like this was easy to extrapolate...

Sadly, the assurance Horus found in his calculations steadily diminished as he went on, until he was left feeling as he had at the onset: There was something they all knew, which he did not...

...Or, maybe a *lot* of somethings. He had a very tough time, trying to sum-up the bits and pieces of conversation he overheard on his way, whether or not he meant to...

"I tell you, she was just milling about, minding her own business, when suddenly they jumped her!" Horus heard, passing one big group of telltales. "A whole squad of policemen! But she'd done nothing!"

"It can't be true! The police don't go around attacking people for no reason."

"Nay, but it *is* true! I know four different people who read it in the paper! What more proof do you need? They're comin' for us, sure as death. You might be next!"

"If the *Baron* doesn't get to you first, that is."

...Shortly after, he brushed by another cluster of people at the foot of a stair in the city's terraces. Their voices were more hushed...

"They say he spends his nights in the deepest, darkest cellar, playing dirges on the organ, all the while plotting his next strike."

"But how would we know? He's not yet spent a night in the castle."

"Oh, but he will, my lad. He *will*."

...And at the top of the rise, where there was a large square, he found a huge gathering, congregated around a posse of Inquisitors...

"People of Jast-Madiir, I beseech you – on behalf of the Inquisition, and for the good of your country – you must desist with this fear and gossipmongering at once, and resume the orderly execution of your duties. Do not be alarmed. There is no cause for unrest."

"So it's all stories, then?" one in the crowd called back. "Just hearsay and rumors? Even the part about the world coming to an end?"

The Inquisitor shook his head. "I did not say *that*. Much of what you've heard is true. And, of course, the fate of the world is forever uncertain. It may very well end. But I fail to see how this in any way diminishes your responsibilities. Whatever else might be in question, I am sure your Czarina's expectations have not changed. So I urge you: Be comforted, or there may be consequences."

...Horus could only blink as he pressed on. Even resolving to avoid the headlines at their most inflammatory, he found he could not avoid the headlines...

As if to drive that point home, he nearly walked right into a billboard, when the man holding it directly in front of him suddenly stopped and turned around. Naturally, it turned out to be the town Onyxadon-sign-guy. But Horus noted that his sign had been dressed up to suit the occasion...

Onyxadon is coming. Maybe tomorrow?

It was enough to make Horus feel thoroughly disgusted by the time he reached the SAPD. He paused and frowned at it for a while, before even *he* decided he'd feel more at ease indoors, out from under the sky. It tasted much too green for his liking today anyway...

"There you are," Deborah called out to him as he entered the lobby. "I was beginning to worry."

"That seems to be the general tenor of things," he quipped, before softening as she approached. "How are you this morning, Deborah? Did you get some decent rest?"

"I only wish I knew," she said, shrugging.

"Horus!" he heard Art call from far away. "There you are!"

Horus took a look at his pocket watch. "There seems to be a lot of excitement over my arrival. Am I late for something?"

"Not really," Deborah replied. "But for those who showed up early, it's been a long wait. Blackforest wants to see us. *All* of us. He won't say why."

"Sounds like trouble," Horus sighed. "Very well; let's not keep ourselves in suspense..."

* * *

They all stood there in silence while Blackforest glowered.

Horus slowly progressed from an attentive look through all manner of fidgety eyes, waiting ever more uncomfortably for the DA to commence whatever browbeating he had in store...

"Something the matter, Hamilton?" he ventured at length.

More glowering.

"...Some unfortunate development overnight?"

Still more glowering.

"...Possibly pertaining to the Tweed case?"

"He *knows*, Templar... as if there could be any doubt," Blucille put in, from down the row. Naturally, they were all lined up to face the firing squad in Blackforest's eyes. "He found out about our snooping at the Embassy."

"Very good, Ms. Cordon," Blackforest intoned, before turning his molten gaze back on Horus. "Imagine my surprise and delight, when I discovered that my own, trusty right hand had willfully capitulated to go behind my back and do *exactly* what I said not to do."

"Now, just a minute Hamilton..." Horus began.

"...I'm not finished," Blackforest silenced him with an upraised claw. "Do you want to know *how* I found out, Horus?"

Horus could only grin and shrug uncomfortably. "I can't imagine."

"No... no you couldn't. Not in a *million* years." He whipped a document up, just in front of Horus' nose. "I got this order from the office of High Constable Amadeus, instructing me to turn Tweed over to his Lieutenant Thermidor."

Horus went utterly blank. Was he dreaming? It was just like a nightmare, jumbling his recent experiences into an incoherent mess. "Constable Amadeus... asked for *Tweed*?"

"Formally collected him might be a better way of putting it."

"But I don't understand. What could possibly be the connection?"

"I'm frankly still working to wrap my head around that myself," Blackforest admitted, turning to Blucille. "Ms. Cordon, why don't you bring your good friend here up to speed? I'm *sure* you can explain it better than I could."

"I'll do my best, Boss," she said sheepishly. They all broke formation enough to attend to what Blucille had to say. "It would seem that our investigation turned up a more shocking discovery than we could've hoped to predict."

"Isn't that just the way?" Blackforest butted back in. "What a shame no one was around to warn you not to stick your nose where it doesn't belong. But I digress. Please, continue."

"Right," Blucille muttered, not making eye contact. "Anyway, to put it as plainly as possible, Sgt. Paprika and his men found Tweed's name on a minute... a minute recording the reading of Carlisle McEnroe's last will and testament."

"Carlisle McEnroe?" Horus asked, doubling down on his incredulous look. "The famous eccentric billionaire?"

"Yes," Blucille nodded. She shrugged apologetically. "Turns out he was Tweed's grandfather."

Horus blinked. "That's... that's very shocking. But it's hardly more than just another fact I can't rationalize. How does this relate back to the High Constable?"

"Well, to understand that, you have to remember the terms of McEnroe's will. It was the subject of quite a lot of gossip at the time... a final oddity to remember the strange old man by."

Horus stroked his chin, working to recall. "Yes... it seems to me he left the bulk of his estate to..." He stopped dead in his tracks as it hit him. "...To his secret grandchild."

Blucille reluctantly confirmed his memory. "That's right."

"But it makes no sense," Deborah interjected. "I mean, clearly we're driving at Tweed coming into McEnroe's fortune, right? But he wouldn't have been a 'secret grandchild' at the time the will was read! The Embassy didn't scrub his family history until earlier this week! Are we supposed to believe McEnroe had Heron powers... that he somehow predicted all this?"

"That's the operative question, Deborah," Blackforest answered. "The only way we can prevent Tweed inheriting billions is to open a cold case. We have to find out who the *real* secret grandchild is... the original one. It's the only way we can prove that McEnroe intended someone besides Tweed to inherit."

"And we would *have to* prove it," Horus mused aloud. "Because as things stand, Tweed equates to the 'secret grandchild' in the eyes of the law. It won't matter how anachronistic it all is. The courts will certainly have to rule that the terms of the will – as read – are satisfied."

Art whistled. "To think of a wacko like Tweed coming into all that cash."

"But then again... he *can't*," Horus came back, realizing something else. "A killer can't inherit. The money would default to..." He reeled as he once again caught up with himself. "It would default to the State."

"That's where the High Constable comes in," Blucille explained. "He was advised of all this... apparently before *I* was. His lieutenant informed us that we've had our chance to solve Tweed's crime. Amadeus has taken matters into his own hands."

"What does *that* mean?" Horus asked, fearing the worst. "Torture, surely. He'll carve Tweed's full confession out of him just the way Nokkaeru suggested. Where have they taken him? I have to see him at once..."

Blackforest waved him down again. "Don't lose your head, Counselor... it's not at all what you think. Quite the opposite, in fact. The High Constable has more compelling means than torture. *Bribery*, I think, would be the word for it."

Horus' face scrunched up. "Bribery? What sort of bribery?"

"Only the best. Promise of a pardon after he's sentenced. And afterwards, a life of luxury and prestige. A life he's enjoying the fruits of even as we speak." Blackforest forced his own most serious look, to be sure Horus didn't take what he was about to say as a joke. "They've given him a Barony, Horus. They took him straight from here to the old Baskervania Manor."

Horus searched Blackforest up and down. It *had* to be a fiction. But of course, he knew it was too weird not to be true. "Unbelievable."

"I can't rectify it either," Blucille commiserated. "Why would the High Constable cook up such a desperate cash-grab in the first place?"

Blackforest and Horus exchanged a knowing, uncomfortable look.

"There are some questions better left unanswered, Ms. Cordon," the voice of Miloje imparted. Horus was surprised to see him leaning on Blackforest's desk, deeper in the room. He hadn't even noticed him before. But then, the DA's sustained glowering had demanded the bulk of his attention.

"What about the Czarina herself?" Art ventured. "Just a couple days ago, she wanted to avoid freaking the public out by turning a killer loose on the Syzygy. Now you're telling me she's supposed to endorse his pardon... even let the Constable make the guy a *Baron*?"

"For a couple billion pence in her treasury?" Blackforest replied. "Yes, I believe she would."

Art shook his head. "But what about the cost? She'd have to fund Tweed's high living out of pocket. Being a Baron isn't cheap."

"Better check your math, Art," Blackforest retorted. "McEnroe's fortune could float a dozen lifetimes of opulence. And, of course, the title costs the Czarina nothing. This would mean a big payday for her, alright."

"My goodness," Horus boded, as he happened on a theory. "Supposing... supposing Tweed killed his grandfather..."

They all looked at him with wide eyes. "Impossible," Blucille said finally. "McEnroe's been dead for years. Those bruises we found all up and down Tweed's arms would've healed long ago. And anyway, his death wasn't ruled suspicious. There was certainly no sign of strangulation."

Horus shook his head. "But the Doctor informed me just last night that the bruises don't actually suggest he strangled anyone. They may have no bearing on the case at all."

The surprised expressions in the room redoubled, as everyone exchanged glances. "We'll unseal the McEnroe file, too," Blackforest sighed. "In the meantime, there's only a hundred other things we need to do to start shoring up this debacle."

Blucille stepped forward. "I *am* sorry I went behind your back, Mr. Blackforest. I accept full responsibility for everything that's happened."

"Yes you do," Blackforest nodded, nevertheless angling a look in Horus' direction. "And so does Horus."

"What do you want us to do?" Horus asked.

"We're splitting up," Blackforest explained. "You'll go with Stenya to Baskervania Manor. See how Amadeus' men have faired with Tweed. Who knows? If all this really was an elaborate scheme to profit by the death of his grandfather, maybe they've got a confession out of him. But based on everything I've seen so far, I doubt it."

"It should be a telling reunion, in any event," Horus replied.

"As for you," Blackforest went on, turning back to Blucille. "You're coming with me to the Embassy."

Blucille looked dumbstruck. "You're going to the Embassy?"

"Yes," Blackforest confirmed. "I'm obliged now to finish what you started. I've already checked into the matter of McEnroe's secret heir, and I think I can put the whole question to rest with just a few well-aimed questions."

"Just a moment..." Horus put in, perplexed. "You want to find the true heir yourself, even knowing how that would tend to frustrate the plans of the High Constable... and even the fortunes of the Czarina?"

Blackforest fired back with another incendiary gaze. "So what if I do? Last time I checked, I'm still the District Attorney of St. Argonsburg, and I'd like to think that counts for something. I have some plans of my own for this city... plans to keep it orderly and respectable... plans that certainly don't involve deferring to a maniac and a killer as *'Lord Baron'*! Anyway, the Czarina still has her 57% Inheritance Tax to cushion the blow. I think that'll have to be good enough."

Horus smiled. "Why, Hamilton... this may be the most leaderly thing you've ever done."

Blackforest returned the grin insincerely. "Horus, I'm already on my third set of furniture in the last week. Don't push it."

Horus cleared his throat. "Well, seeing as you've laid out the plan, I suppose it's time to be moving on anyway." He bobbed his chin at Miloje. "Are you ready to go, Milo?"

"I'll be along presently," Miloje replied. "You go ahead. It should be no trouble catching up with you."

"Well for goodness' sake, let's none of us dawdle," Blackforest instructed. "Tweed, the presses, reality itself... they've all had one too many laughs at our expense. It's time we settled the score. We'll show them. We'll put a stop to all this madness. And we'll do it by midnight tonight."

* * *

"Arcadian Tweed – a Baron," Deborah recounted as she and Horus went barreling down the halls of Civil Headquarters. "What's the world coming to?"

"Possibly a premature end, if I overheard the morning gossip correctly," Horus replied.

"At this point that would just about figure," she quipped.

"Not to worry. Seems to me there's a prominent Heron prophecy or two still unfulfilled... though none spring to mind at the moment. I think the world will go on. More importantly, we have a plausible new theory to investigate." He grinned at her confidently. "And, we have the rest of the day."

"*'Plausible'* hasn't done us much good so far..." She angled a quizzical expression at him. "You really mean to hold yourself to Blackforest's midnight deadline? I mean, do you think it's important we pin down Tweed before the Syzygy crests?"

He shrugged. "I can certainly see merit in it. The people seem to think our entire administration has been reduced to a mere cog in a cosmic system of chaos. If Tweed can be properly indited before the high point of the Syzygy, then hopefully that will suffice to reassure them that their fears were never more than silly superstition."

"Right," she said. "So how do you want to attack this?"

"As ordered by Hamilton. I'm going to see Tweed straight away." He looked over at her again. "But I want you to stay here and see what comes when they dig up McEnroe's death record. We should certainly have the hard facts, in the likely case Tweed remains uncooperative."

"A royal pain, you mean."

"Almost too on the nose, all things considered."

She nodded. "Well, I don't need any convincing to stay behind. That castle gave me the creeps long before it was the den of a psycho."

"Fair enough. We'll debrief later."

She gave him a small wave as their paths began to fork. "Alright. Good luck, Boss."

"To both of us."

* * *

Just when he was beginning to think he'd missed her entirely, Art spied Deborah on her way down to Archives. He stepped out in front of her, along with Blucille and Captain Alexei...

"Heya, Debs..." he said, running a hand across the back of his neck, apologetic from the start. "We... that is, *I*... wanted to say I was sorry for what happened last night in your yard."

"You can certainly say, *'we,'* Mr. Mallard," Alexei put in. "We are all of us ashamed for that shoddy bit of work."

"What are you talking about?" Deborah asked. "What happened in my yard?" She looked between all of them before her eyes came to rest on Art again. "And what are *they* doing here with you?"

"Heh, well, ya see..." Art stumbled.

"Ugh, I knew this was a mistake!" Blucille burst. "Clearly she slept right through the whole thing! We're just digging ourselves deeper every way we turn."

"It is no mistake to be forthright and apologize, Ms. Cordon," Alexei argued.

"*Art*," Deborah rejoined through her teeth. "*What* are they doing here?"

"Okay, *fine*!" Blucille huffed. "Deborah, I'm sorry. This is really my fault. I pressured Art into explaining everything."

Deborah stared daggers at Art. "*Everything*?"

"Yeah," he shrugged, grinning like a buffoon. "I gave them the whole Werehuman story. So really it's me who should be accepting all the blame."

"Yet let us not forget, that it was *I* who tackled that poor unsuspecting woman," Alexei lamented. "Surely that was the greatest unkindness to come of this whole misadventure."

"You... he...?" Deborah reeled. "Art, telling Blucille is one thing... if I didn't see *that* one coming, I have no one to blame but myself. But how is *Captain Alexei* a part of all this?!"

"Well, I figured we needed him in case we had to arrest you. We even thought we *did* for a minute there! Only, it turned out to be some random lady by the name of 'Hailey Barborough'."

For a moment, Deborah could only blink. "This is like a nightmare that just won't end," she said.

"And yet, perhaps it is coming to a head," another voice intruded. They all whirled, and there was Miloje...

"*Deputy Constable*," Alexei choked out, horrified.

"Hey now," Art said, pointing a finger. "Where did you come from?"

Miloje turned his hands up. "I used to have some skill at covert operations, before my decline. I had a mind to get back into practice. It would seem my efforts are not wasted." He shook his head, looking most unimpressed. "Imagine my own surprise, learning so much from one quiet stroll. I myself had dismissed the story about a policeman bowling over a random pedestrian as an obvious fiction. I had no intention of even looking into it. Until now."

Blucille quickly stepped out into the gulf between the Deputy Constable and her co-conspirators. "Miloje, I..."

"You what?" he interjected. "You want to take full responsibility again? Too bad. I have no authority to discipline *you*. Nor do I have any wish to discover what would happen if Blackforest learned of a second grievous misjudgment on your part in the same day."

She looked down, even as Miloje angled past her at Art. "As for you: You're off this case! *Both* cases: Ms. Boulevard's and the Tweed investigation. You're off *every* case until this Syzygy nonsense has passed! I have more than a sneaking suspicion that I have you to thank for the bombastic headlines of late. Shape up! And see that you lose your tail, if you ever want to consult with this department again!"

Art looked dejectedly at the ground, too. "Roger that, Skipper," he sighed.

Miloje's steely eyes softened as he turned to Deborah. "Now, Ms. Boulevard: It seems plain to me that you are no more than the victim of this half-baked operation. I sympathize with your plight. If you wish, I can arrange for you to spend the next few nights in security. I can put your house under the vigil of a whole team of highly-trained officers... ones who know how to practice *real* discretion."

She grinned weakly. "Thank you, Milo. I may take you up on that."

"Let me know what you decide," he replied. Then, he turned to go. "Meantime, we all have places to be."

"But Sir!" Alexei protested. "You haven't said what you intend to do with *me* yet!"

Miloje froze. He turned back only a few degrees... not enough to really see his face, though it was clear that he was seething. "When I've decided what to do, you'll be hearing from me," he boded. "Until then, let your imagination run wild. I certainly intend to." And then, he walked away.

"Oh, poo," Alexei said, once Miloje had quite gone. He slumped and sighed, turning slowly to go. "Perhaps I should find Captain Brocksmith straight away – congratulate him on the surety of his promotion."

"I'm right there with you, Alexei," Blucille commiserated, shuffling away in similar fashion. "If I've so much as kept the boss waiting, I've had it."

...That left Art and Deborah...

"Sorry," Art said at length.

Deborah waved it off. "It's alright. I'm just numb to it now."

"Hey," he said, stopping her just before she made her own dejected exit. He looked seriously at her. "I'll find a way to make it up to you. Pinky promise."

She sighed. "No, Art, please. Just do what Miloje said and let's be done with this. That's really the best thing you can do for me now."

Art took her tired resignation like a punch to the gut as she walked away. He'd failed her, and the price was high. She'd obviously lost all faith in him...

But he was no quitter... and a pinky promise was a pinky promise...

He'd find a way to cheer her up yet...

Chapter 14

As the carriage inched past the crusty gates, Horus heard the horses whinny their dismay. He stuck his nose out the window, resolving to see for himself the desolation that lay ahead. The sight was indeed unpleasant.

Baskervania Manor – a defiant slab on the horizon, jutting out of a heap of pulverized earth and looking twice as old. It was the last keepsake of an unfortunate era before taxes had been properly federalized – a monument to surly feudal lords that would otherwise have been happily forgotten long ago. To that end, it seemed that even the land itself was up in arms to reclaim the ancient fort. The place was covered in meaty vines, wrenching down on the walls for all they were worth. But the Manor refused to relent, merely chipping away here and there every few centuries, and then only as a calculated measure to intensify its own ugliness.

"What a mess," Horus said. He turned back in to look at Miloje. "How long do you suppose it's been since someone lived here?"

The Deputy Constable shrugged. "*Lived*? I could hardly speculate. But I'm given to understand that the royal family condemned the estate nearly two hundred years ago. And that was only after they had ceased using it for holiday or putting up foreign dignitaries for generations. Baskervania Manor is quite thoroughly disused."

"It shows," Horus quipped, eyeing the castle again with a frown. "I hate to admit it, but the place rather suits Tweed... in a macabre sort of way."

Miloje huffed. "I don't see how. It's much too good for him."

Horus shook his head. "You really deplore the man, don't you?"

"Of course. Do you mean to say you don't?"

"Well, to be fair, he *is* one of the most infuriating people I've ever met," Horus admitted. "But I do my best to pity him. It really is a shame that anyone should have to be so detached from reality."

"You surprise me, Templar. Hardly an hour ago, you posited that Tweed may well have killed his own grandfather with hopes of coming into a fortune. Isn't that rather too shrewd and calculating for a deranged man?"

"On the contrary," Horus challenged. "I would say the man who would kill for material gain is the most deranged kind there is."

"Fair enough. But you'll forgive me if I don't share in your pity. Few will be so pleased as I to see him get what's coming to him."

* * *

They were shown through a foyer of cobwebs and a tangled courtyard of mutilated statues before ascending a stair to an oversize second story. Here, they came face-to-face with a vast wall that stretched featureless into complete dark on either side. There was only one door they could see, and it was directly in front of them. They were content to wait for the soldier – one of Lieutenant Thermidor's men – to open it...

As the door swung, it opened into a large parlor, loosing a powerful, acrid smell. Horus and Miloje walked slowly in, their eyes drawn directly to the raised dais at the far side of the room, where quivering torchlight kept the shadows churning at a distance on the moth-eaten tapestries. They approached the short stair, passing rows of ancient harps with broken, curling strings. And at the top, between armed guards and a small host of servants, was Tweed, presiding over his own gilded cage, casting a big, stupid grin down at them as he sat on his throne.

"Well, hi there, Mr. Templar!" he said. "Fancy meeting you here!"

"Hello, Tweed," Horus grudged.

"*Tweed*, did you say?" he repeated. He went on to tsk at them. "You're going to have to be a little more formal than that from now on, Mr. Templar. It's *Baron Von Tweed*, to the likes of you."

"*Von* Tweed? Now just where did the *Von* come from?"

"From the same place the *Baron* did, of course," Tweed shrugged. "You obviously don't know how these old titles work." He sat up straighter and commenced bouncing. "You see? I get this big chair..." He stopped, and gestured for a woman in his retinue to come to his side. "And I get this lady to feed me grapes." He took a mouthful, chewing disgustingly. "You want some? They're pretty good, even with the smokey aftertaste."

"We didn't come to eat grapes with you," Horus explained, his patience already fraying. "We came to collect your overdue confession."

"Ah yes... *we*..." Tweed said, turning a frown at Miloje. "I did notice you brought 'Junior' with you. Must be 'bring-your-kid-to-work-day' again or something." He snapped his fingers. "Somebody got a lollipop and a pat on the head for the little guy?"

"Upon my word!" Miloje grumbled, turning up an accusatory finger. "We've had quite enough of this before! How is it that someone as unbolted as you could come to be utterly fixated on the idea that I am no more than a minor?"

"Now, now! What would your mother think if she heard you talking to your Baron that way?"

"My *mother* indeed! I'll show you what *I* think of...!"

"...Milo!" Horus interjected. "We're not here to argue about nothing. If you can't hold it back then maybe it's best if you wait outside the parlor."

"Very good, Mr. Templar," Tweed said, offering light applause. "A little time-out is just what the brat's asking for."

Miloje boiled. But then, he straightened up, plastering-on a vehement grin. "I think I'll do one better and wait in the carriage. But mark this, *Baron*: the next time I see this loathsome place, you'll be coming back to Headquarters with me."

"That'll be a cold day in the tropics, Tiny Tim," Tweed egged him on. Even so – and in spite of everything in his nature – Miloje removed himself without another word...

"Boy, I'm glad *he's* gone," Tweed quipped, reclining over the arms of his throne as he waved the grape lady back over. "Now I can get back to Baroning in peace."

"Tweed..." Horus began to appeal.

But Tweed upraised a finger. "*Von* Tweed."

"Right," Horus agreed half-heartedly. "You *do* understand the terms of this... this royal appointment of yours... don't you? Did the High Constable and his men explain it to you adequately?"

Tweed nodded. "Sure they did. I tell them who I killed, and I get to keep this nifty old castle. It's like a gift exchange. Simple as pie."

"...*Have* you told them, then?" Horus asked.

"*Pfft...*" Tweed replied. "No."

"Why haven't you?" Horus demanded. "You must also understand: If you fail to meet their terms, all of this goes away. They'll take back the castle, the Barony, and everything."

Tweed shrugged. "So let 'em. I didn't ask for this. I wanted something practical. Like a yo-yo."

Horus brushed his head. "I can't figure you, Baron Von Tweed. What happened to your aspirations? What happened to the dream of the Old Miser? Don't you see? You're getting that dream right now... whether by diabolical calculation or the most absurd twist of fate I've ever heard of. You mustn't let it slip away! You can't!"

"Sure I can," he smiled. "It's easy."

Horus balled his fists. He forced himself to breathe. Then, he remembered his new angle. It was time to try it out...

"Supposing... supposing I were to tell you that I *know* who it is you killed."

Tweed laughed out loud. "Then I would laugh right in your face. Just like this!"

"Would you really, though... if I was right?" Horus challenged. "What if I told you, you killed your rich grandfather?"

Tweed's laughter slowly faded as his face began to scrunch. "You mean Grandpappy McEnroe? That's silly! I wouldn't kill *him*. He had a polka dotted night cap."

Horus shook his head. "You're not going to dodge the question so easily this time," he cautioned. "If I'm right, there's a method to your madness. I think you devised a way to inherit his estate. A way to take that polka dotted night cap for your own... along with everything else! You killed him and got away with it. You went on to make yourself a byword at the Embassy, until, by the time word of your crime came out, they wanted nothing more than to disown you... to erase all record of you. And in so doing they made your relationship to your own grandfather a secret, inadvertently setting you up as the heir apparent to his marooned fortune! And now, here we are... with the State prepared to grant you a life of luxury so you'll default on your inheritance!"

Tweed went blank. "That doesn't make any sense. Even to *me*."

Horus regarded him with narrow eyes. "You deny killing your grandfather, then?"

"Yup."

"Then prove it. Name the *real* victim."

"Nope."

"*Who* did you kill, Tweed?" Horus insisted, an edge coming into his voice. "How did you do it? Did you use a gun?"

"Are you kidding? I would never kill someone with a gun."

"Why not? Do you have something against guns?"

"Oh no, not at all! I think guns are awesome! It's bullets I don't like."

"Very well. If not a gun, then what was it? A knife?"

"No."

"A fireplace poker?"

"No."

"A wooden mallet?"

"No."

"A club? A pike? A stick? A fence post? A banjo, a trebuchet, a weaver's rod?! A dead *fish*?! What was it, Tweed? What *was* it?!!"

"No, no, no, no, *no*, *NO*, ***NO***!" Tweed exclaimed, smashing his hand into the arm of his throne with ever-greater strength.

Horus looked on, just as if drawn into a trance. A flashback of Tweed's testimony on the stand played out in his mind. "I DID IT, I DID IT, I DID IT!!" He'd slammed his protest onto the bench with that same crushing force...

"...Alright," Horus assented at length. "I can see you're still loath to come clean on this. But I'm warning you... you're running out of chances. Even as we speak, Carlisle McEnroe's death record is being recovered from the archives. If there was anything suspicious about the circumstances – anything at all – you may well find yourself being arraigned on his murder regardless."

Tweed, calming down, offered no immediate answer. But the more he relaxed, the more he began to look confident again. Invincibly, hideously confident...

"Okay," he finally said. "But you're *cold*, Mr. Templar. And getting colder."

Horus struggled to retain an impassive front. He slowly started backpedaling to the door. "I'm leaving, Baron," he cautioned. "This might be your last chance to speak your piece. When I walk out this door... you may not see me again until I'm representing you in court."

Tweed waved goodbye. "Okeedoke. See you there!"

Horus was finally forced to turn and walk away. He held his breath for a moment, hoping against hope that the sight of his back might inspire some doubt in Tweed. He paused at the door. He turned back. "This is it, Tweed. One more step and I'm gone."

"Ah-ah! *Baron Von* Tweed," the crazy little man corrected.

"*Right*," Horus agreed again. He very slowly closed the door behind him. When it latched, he put his ear up against it. He listened intently. But no one called after him...

...He walked down the stairs, back out into the creepy courtyard... totally defeated...

* * *

"Don't look so pleased with yourself, Templar," Miloje called out, before Horus even realized his slow shuffle had brought him nearly to the door of the police carriage. "It's unbecoming."

"I really grilled him on McEnroe, Stenya," Horus sighed, climbing in. "But it was fruitless. He honestly looked completely blindsided by the suggestion."

"Too bad. But surely, you're not surprised."

"No, not surprised. Though no less disappointed. More than that, now I'm worried. What if we *do* end up pinning the rational murder on the irrational man? What if we convict him of the wrong crime?"

Miloje shook his head. "You're diving too deep, Counselor. What difference does it make who he killed, in the end? We know he killed *someone*. He should pay for it accordingly."

"I suppose..." Horus went along weakly. "At any rate, I seem to have failed my mission. I hope Hamilton fares better..."

Chapter 15

Blackforest tugged out his jacket as he marched on the wide court in all its livery. A vast, encircling embrasure between the arched wings of the Embassy flew the flags of just about every country known to the civilized world. And immediately ahead of him, at the far side of the courtyard, was a forked pole of special prominence, naturally flying Jast-Madiir's colors high above the rest... and on much, much bigger canvas. His vision darkened as he drew under it, reaching for the doorway. He opened it, gesturing for Blucille to go in first. He listened as her small feet clicked faster on the stone while she hurried past, eyes down. She'd lost a few steps on him since the carriage. She seemed to be scrambling to keep up, and clearly was a bit uncomfortable for it. Good.

The receptionists behind the sweeping front desk took immediate notice of their arrival, even through all the diverse passersby in the lobby. They appeared a little daunted, or even apprehensive. That was also just as it should be. If Blackforest was a bit given to projecting when his dander was up, it tended to have the upshot of inspiring responsiveness in people around him...

"Welcome to the Embassy, Sir, Ma'am," one of them greeted sheepishly. "Can I get your names, so that I can help you fill out your guest badges?"

"Hamilton Blackforest, and this is Blucille Cordon," Blackforest answered.

"You're the District Attorney?" she asked, her grey face bleaching. "I... I take it you're here for more on the Baron? The Syzygy Ki...?"

"...The Arcadian Tweed investigation, yes," he interrupted.

The receptionist commenced hurried scratching, pen in hand. "I can personally take you anywhere on the grounds you mean to go, Sir, as soon as your badge is in order. But I'm afraid you've already subpoenaed all our records. I don't know if there's anything more for you to learn here. Certainly not from the archives."

"That's no issue. I'm here to see Broach Vandon and Yolonda Jeffries."

He watched her eyes dart quizzically, but she looked up just long enough to nod. And then, after hardly another moment of flurried jotting, she stood up. "Pin these on please, and I'll show you to them."

* * *

Standing outside an unmarked apartment within the complex with their names hanging in a long list of languages from their jackets, Blackforest and Blucille let the receptionist knock on the door. In short order, they were let in by Yolonda, and shown the living room in the back, where her husband Broach sat. Also present was a quiet, unassuming pre-teen girl, doodling on the floor...

"Broach, this is District Attorney Hamilton Blackforest, and his Assistant, Blucille Cordon," Yolonda introduced them.

Broach got up and shook their hands. "Glad to meet you," he said... though his discomfort was pungent. "I suppose you're here about my nephew."

"You could say that," Blackforest answered. "No doubt you've heard how the rediscovery of his family ties has come with some rather unfortunate consequences. But I'm hopeful that – in just a short visit – you might be able to help the State sort this whole thing out." His look moved studiously toward the girl.

Broach didn't reply at once, instead crouching down by the youth. "Tilda, Honey... your adoptive mother and I – your adoptive father, that is – we're going to do some grown-up talking with these people from the police department. Would you like to go out and feed the birds for a bit?"

She looked up at him with questioning eyes. "Grown-up talk? Daddy, I'm almost twelve... practically the age of majority. I can handle mature conversation! Can't I just stay inside and throw paper airplanes around?"

"Please, Dear," Yolonda insisted. "Just let us handle this in private."

The girl's shoulders dropped as she relented. "Oh, okay."

"Thank you, adoptive daughter," Broach said after her as she walked to the door, and then out. Then, he turned to Blackforest. "Alright, now. What is it you want to know about Arcadian? We've never been that close, mind you, but I'll gladly share anything I know."

Blackforest chuckled a bit deviously. "That's a leading question, Mr. Vandon. I don't have anything to ask about Tweed himself. Or, if I do, it would only be this: Do you honestly believe your father, Carlisle McEnroe, wrote his will with any hope or expectation of Tweed inheriting his estate?"

Broach Vandon looked to his wife, obviously wishing for some way to avoid answering. "No," he finally admitted. "No, I'm quite sure he didn't."

"And how is it you can be so sure?" Blackforest pressed him.

Broach doubled down on his retentiveness. He forced a long, uneasy breath through his nose, before he slowly crossed the room, casting his gaze out a large window in the back, overlooking a fenced-off little yard. He watched Tilda for a while, pouring seeds into a series of feeders, with birds all around tweeting their excitement.

"She seems sweet – your adoptive daughter," Blackforest commented as they all gathered by the window. "Intelligent, too. Perhaps even a bit mysterious. Did you know, Mr. Vandon, that prior to your adopting her, we can find no record of Tilda at all? No birth certificate? No prior citizenship?"

Broach shrugged. "The paperwork must not've made it on the boat with us."

"Now, that's a *glaring* misconstrual of the facts," Blackforest replied. "I don't believe she came here on any boat... and I know for a fact that *you* didn't. Your father was hardly even of marrying age when *he* came over. Your birth happened right *here*, and it's well documented. So now, how do you account for Tilda's missing paper trail?"

The man shook his head. "Maybe I can't. How is it my problem if these things get misplaced? Our adoption papers are in order; that's all that concerns me."

Blackforest frowned. "Mr. Vandon: I wouldn't put me to the test right now, if I were you. It's obvious you know something you're not telling. I can smell it. Don't force me to play hardball to get it out of you."

Broach regarded him defiantly. "What do you think you can do to me? I didn't commit any crime."

"Destroying public records *is* a crime, Mr. Vandon," he fired back. "Oh, maybe you don't think I can prove you did. But frankly, I wouldn't have to. There are other ways I could make trouble for you, if you choose to be uncooperative."

"What do you mean?"

"Well, seeing as we've already opened the door, let's take a closer look at your roots," Blackforest said, interlacing his claws in front of him. "Your father wasn't sent here as any ambassador or emissary, Mr. Vandon. To my knowledge, he neglected to ever so much as mention where it was he came from in the first place. Nevertheless, his vast wealth proved enough to reserve a place for him here, among our most prominent foreign dignitaries... no questions asked. And with respect to that fortune, the same privilege seems to have been extended to your brother and his family... and you and yours. That puts you on pretty shaky ground, if you ask me. In fact,

I'd say your comfortable lodgings here are the result of an oversight, at best. An accounting error."

Broach's eyes bugged. "You'd... you'd have us thrown out of the Embassy, just to get at the truth about Tilda?"

"Let me to rephrase that for you," Blackforest answered. "Are you really prepared to face losing your home, just to protect her secret?"

Mr. Vandon turned away again, deliberating.

"It's not as if we've lied," Yolonda piped up, while she reached out and put a hand on her husband's shoulder. "We *did* adopt her. That should be enough."

"It should be, but it isn't."

Blackforest turned back to Broach Vandon.

He remained silent for a moment... building to the operative question...

"Who did you adopt her *from*?"

"We..." Broach began to answer, his voice filled with pain. "We adopted her from ourselves."

Blackforest turned to Blucille, taking a moment to enjoy the look of surprise in her eyes. He only grinned at her, before returning to Broach...

"That's just what I thought," he said. "And that makes Tilda the true heir. The intended one."

"You certainly seemed to have some idea when you came in here," Broach nodded with his eyes down, still filled with emotion from dredging up such a deep, dark secret. "What on earth made you suspect? What gave us away?"

"It was just the simplest way to reconcile all the facts," Blackforest explained. "McEnroe knew he had a secret grandchild. So naturally, I had to look at his only children... his two sons. When I saw that one of you had an adoptive daughter with no preexisting paper trail, well... that made for one too many mysteries. But I got to thinking: What if one mystery solves the other? What if it turns out his secret grandchild has been hidden in plain sight all along?"

"Well, you're certainly a shrewd one, Mr. Blackforest... I'll give you that." His sad eyes wandered back through the glass, settling lovingly on his biological, adoptive daughter. "But in a way, I suppose I'm grateful to you. It's been very hard on us... on *all* of us, keeping the truth under wraps. Surely Tilda herself has suffered the most for it." He blinked back tears, shaking his head. "When I think of all the years she's lost, never knowing that she was being raised by her own parents. We *wanted* to tell her, of course. We were in agony to tell her the truth. But we couldn't."

"Why not?" Blucille suddenly ventured.

"We..." Broach began, finger extended, before coming to an abrupt halt. "Well, I mean, *obviously*, we couldn't just..." he tried a second time. Once again, the man and his wife exchanged looks. This time though, their eyes were not pained or reserved. More like, they were blank. "Hmm..." the man answered at length, scratching his chin, while they both went on racking their brains...

"Well, never mind," Blackforest suggested. "The truth is out now, and that's all that matters. I think it's high time you had a talk with your daughter, and let the healing start to take its course. It should be very good for all of you."

Broach and Yolonda smiled through misty eyes. "Thank you, Mr. Blackforest," the woman replied. "We'll do just that."

"There is, of course, one other matter," he reminded them. "The *real* matter that brings me here in the first place."

"Yes... of course," Broach sniffled, wiping his nose. "You'll want us to come forward and settle my father's estate properly."

"I'm *counting* on you to do that," Blackforest intoned. "The city of St. Argonsburg itself is counting on you."

Broach drew his wife into an embrace as he nodded. "We will. I'm sure it's the least we can do." He laughed. "Imagine my dad... leaving all his money to a 'secret grandchild'. Honestly, Mr. Blackforest... with all due respect to my old man... he really *was* kind of a nut. Thank goodness Arcadian was the only one in the family to take after him."

"I wonder," Blucille interjected before she thought better of it.

Blackforest set his hand on her shoulder, guiding her to the exit. "Come now, Ms. Cordon. Our work here is finally done."

* * *

The occasional look at his Assistant District Attorney confirmed: The ride back to Civil HQ was perhaps even more uncomfortable for Blucille than the ride to the Embassy had been. Blackforest was content to let her stew in it for a while longer. But after they'd climbed one particularly steep grade, he decided it was finally time to engage her...

"You're quiet, Ms. Cordon," he said. "*Too* quiet. Come on, now... you're not going to let one little reckoning take all the starch out of you forever, are you?"

"I guess I'm still waiting for the actual reckoning," she answered. "I really blew it this time; there's no two ways about it. I defied your orders. I attempted to deceive you. I assumed I knew better, and I couldn't have been more disastrously wrong."

"That's very true," he nodded. "You didn't behave like an Assistant District Attorney at all." He folded his arms as he leaned back into the seat of the carriage, taking on a more informal air. "However... you're not just my Assistant, are you? You're also my *student*. You're training under me to become a full District Attorney yourself, some day in the far-flung future. And, when I consider how you performed in that capacity – as a District Attorney – I don't think you really did so bad."

She eyed him suspiciously. "How do you figure that?"

"Well, you made your own judgment call. You showed autonomy. You went looking for the facts, even when it meant taking a serious risk. And when it all caved in on you, you tried to take full accountability... even though we both know it was Horus who instigated the whole thing. Now make no mistake: As your boss, I *am* disappointed in you. But as your teacher, well... I'm almost a little proud."

She grinned sheepishly. "That's nice. I'll try to bear that in mind through the worst of whatever disciplinary measures you decide to take."

He shook his head. "Blucille, this *was* your discipline."

She looked at him again like he was spouting crazy talk. "What? *This*? You rolled in and fixed everything I royally messed up while I just sat around like a useless dunderhead and watched!"

Blackforest nodded. "Exactly."

She paused, contemplating. "Well, that's rather unconventional. But you know, it kind of works."

"On anyone that holds themselves to a reasonable standard, yes... I think it does."

She sighed. "Well, that makes me feel a lot better about the future."

"We're not out of the woods yet," Blackforest boded. "We're going to have to hit the ground running when we get back to Headquarters, if we want to unseat the Baron by midnight. Which we *do*."

"Is it really so important?" Blucille asked. "I mean, aren't we on the verge of acting a bit superstitiously ourselves?"

"Open your window," Blackforest instructed.

Blucille slid the curtain open, revealing the wide world of commuters just outside.

"You smell that fear?" he asked.

She shrugged. "Honestly, my nose has been on the fritz all day."

"Well, you can see them clustering into gossip groups, can't you?"

"*Yes*," she sighed tiredly.

"Okay then. I'm not above admitting I was wrong... on occasion. If we wait until the Syzygy is waning to put Tweed in his place, we don't just give the people license to hold onto their paranoia... we miss our only chance to *prove* they had the wrong idea all along. We lose credibility we might not be able to win back for the next half-dozen astronomical events." He shrugged. "You can accuse me of being superstitious, if you feel you must. But at the end of the day, I'm first and foremost a pragmatist."

"That's good enough for me," she went along. "I guess I just wanted to reassure myself that we weren't getting as paranoid as the rest of them."

"Of course we're not," Blackforest asserted... half-growling, half snickering. "The Syzygy is total bunk. Anyone with a lick of sense knows it." Suddenly, he shivered... aware for the first time of the temperature. "Now close that blind back up, would you? It's getting a little nippy out."

Chapter 16

"Naw, that was before the 7th District got split up inta 7-A an' 7-B," Eb glacially expounded to his captive audience. "Course, nowadays, ya got 7-C an' 7-D in there, too... but thet's a coon's age removed from what I was a-drivin' at..." He paused to stroke his whiskers thoughtfully. "Huh... now thet's a funny thing. I plum forgot what it *was* I was gittin' around to!"

"Something about complications you've faced in the past regarding regional bylaws," Horus reminded him wearily. He had his head rested on his hands as he stared deep into an imaginary abyss for perhaps the fifth hour in a row.

"Ah... thet's right!" Eb recalled, pleased as a pickle. "I r'member this one time, a feller walked right in thet door an' said..."

"...Excuse me, Eb... I don't mean to interrupt your thought," Deborah interjected. "But I think I should remind everyone that we were supposed to be talking about *Horus'* case... the one he's currently working on. It's rather important that we try to solve it in the very near future."

"It's also completely useless," Horus said, blinking a lethargic blink.

They all looked at him incredulously: Eb, Deborah, and Art, who'd also been waylaid. "Now come on Horus; you shouldn't talk like that," Art reprimanded him.

"Shouldn't I?" Horus challenged, sluggishly turning his head. "We've been beating our heads against this Tweed mystery the last three days, and where has it gotten us? Sure, we *had* a suspected victim... for about fifteen minutes. So much for a breakthrough."

"We're quite sure McEnroe's death was natural, then?" Art asked.

Deborah nodded. "The record was plain: death by slow dehydration. Apparently he refused to drink anything but cocktail sauce the last three years of his life."

"Wow," Art replied. "That really *doesn't* leave much room for foul play, does it?"

"And outside of that, all we've managed to do is impeach the one bit of physical evidence we thought we had to go on," Horus bemoaned. "We know less than we did at the beginning. I call that rather hopeless."

"I r'spectfully disagree, Sir," Eb said, drawing himself up stern. "Don't never forget: it ain' a step backwards when ya figures out thet you was goin' the wrong way ta start with." He slowly shook his head. "I's always sayin':

The problem with youngin's is they's always rushin' headlong inta ev'rything."

...He rapped his fist on the desk...

"Ain't *nobody* in this business what can afford ta assume a durn thing. Ya can't take *nothin'* for granted."

...His fist struck again on the word *'nobody'*...

...And again, on the word, *'nothin'*...

The poundings on the desk – though each of them was lethargic and ultimately harmless – might as well have been hammer-strokes in Horus' mind. As each one fell, Horus involuntarily replayed the action of Tweed striking the bench – then the arm of his throne. He saw that noodly little arm slamming down recklessly – *injuriously* – over and over. And suddenly, with bruising forcefulness, it all made sense...

Horus leapt to his feet. "*I can't take anything for granted,*" he chanted quietly to himself. "But of course. That's *it*! We've all been operating on one main assumption from the very beginning. One irrational, impossibly hasty assumption..."

"Whassat, Horus?" Eb inquired, cupping his hand to his folded ear. "If y's havin' one o' them 'epiphetical' moments – the way it looks like y'are – yer gonna have ta speak up. Ma old ears don't work so well anymore."

Horus whirled over to the senior Public Defender, seizing his hand and shaking it. "Eb Thalymus, you've solved the case of the dubious decedent! You're a rare outspoken genius, and a credit to our profession!"

Eb's eyes bugged as Horus sent his whole arm flopping. *"Jumpin' Jiminys,"* he marveled. "I really must'a said somethin'. But what in tarnation did I say?"

"I'll explain it later," Horus replied, with one arm already through the sleeve of his overcoat as he now stood in the doorway. "I have a horrible wrong to right, and a reign of terror to cut short! More than that: I have a client to defend. And no matter how he may try, he can't stop me anymore." He threw the door open, and immediately vanished into the gathering dusk. He left everyone silent, staring...

"Well I'll be..." Eb said at length. He looked at Deborah, and then at Art. His eyes shifted between them a few times, appearing filled with great doubt, like he'd come up on a situation he'd never once faced before. "Sounds like we gone an' had us a major breakthrough here, ladies an' gents. I'd shore love ta sit up an' chat a while... celebrate the occasion proper like. But, then agin..." He stopped, slowly walking away. Then, as a grin curled his jowls, he breathed a contented sigh. "...Maybe I jist orta quit while I'm ahead..."

The door closed behind him, leaving the room in a second stunned silence.

Finally, Art smirked at Deborah, who frowned tiredly back...

"Well, don't just smile like that," Deborah said at length. "What are you so pleased about?"

"Two things," Art revealed. "One: We came out alive on the other side of another Eb lecture. And the second is: I figured out how to pay you back for all the trouble I caused you."

"Great," she intoned. "I don't suppose you'd care to warn me ahead of time what you have in mind?"

"Nope. But trust me: You're gonna like it."

She shrugged. "If you say so."

Art regarded her with concern. "What's a matter, Debs? Eb turned in early; sounds like Horus just cracked his case. But you're still all dumpy. Why's that? Are you still trying to decide whether to spend the night under house arrest?"

She shook her head. "There's no way I'm sleeping tonight anyway."

"Then what?"

She sighed. "Well, as far as I know, there may be only one man left in all of Jast-Madiir who doesn't know my secret. I can't help feeling it's inevitable now."

"Then maybe he should hear it from you," Art suggested.

"Right," she agreed with obvious sarcasm. "Trade my fear he'll find out I'm superstitious for the certainty. Art, we've been over this."

"We have. And I still think I've got the right idea." He suddenly looked about the room, appearing perplexed. "Speaking of Horus... were we supposed to follow him?"

She shook her head. "He would've said so."

"You're sure we shouldn't?" he pressed.

"I know one thing for certain: I'm not going out under those planets tonight unless I have no other choice."

"Fair enough," he went along. "Looks like a cold one anyway. Unseasonably cold..." He got up and crossed to the wall of the car. At close range, his eyes confirmed what his mind could hardly reckon. He turned around, wearing a mystified expression. "The windows are frosting."

* * *

Horus rubbed his hands together, watching and listening with great intent for the next cab. He was far too keyed-up to much notice the sky as it beamed all its brightest shades of black, or even the dazzling invisibility of the borealis that now stretched from World to World. Even so, a moment more spent waiting out there in the elements, and he might've consciously asked himself whether he'd ever been so cold in his life. The answer would've been no.

But he heard the tell-tale pitter-patter of horse's hooves coming around the corner. Rather than wait at the stop, he dashed to intercept...

"Excuse me, Sir!" he called out to the driver. "Excuse me! I'm in great need of your haste; I have urgent business at Baskervania Manor."

The driver looked horrified. "Where did you say? *Baskervania*? You want me to take you *there... **now***?"

"I'm very sorry," Horus said. "I'd make it well worth your while if I could, but I know gratuities would only complicate your income taxes."

"Creators save me!" he exclaimed. "Out of all the cabbies in all of St. Argonsburg..."

"Don't worry," Horus tried. "If we hurry, I can end this tonight. I can end it *all*."

"I'm sure that's exactly what you mean to do," the driver replied in a quavering voice. "But what choice do I have?! Climb in."

* * *

Passably warmer within the closed- off coach, Horus reviewed the data over and over again, searching for any fault in his theory. It was the only thing he could do to fill the seemingly endless ride. He mastered his anxious energy time and again by crunching the data. But every time it came out just the same as his gut had told him it should, he returned to himself, and found that the trot of the horses was surely much too relaxed...

"Faster, please," he called out, trying to maintain some politeness. "This is really very important."

"We're almost there, Sir," the driver called back. "But..."

Horus felt immediately stymied by the man's weak, stunted appeal. "But what? What's the matter?"

"There's..." he started again. "There's something I think you ought to see, Sir. An oddity in the sky..."

Horus rolled his eyes. "I know the planets are in line tonight. Don't let it trouble you. It's really quite unimportant."

"It's not that, Sir. It's... well, it's something else."

With a labored sigh, Horus leaned over and opened his curtain. For a moment after, he was breathless, seeing that the air all around him was positively filled with a gently-wafting stuff so foreign – so mythic in this part of the world – that it commanded his astonishment...

"What in the Undervoid?"

* * *

When the castle was at last in sight, Horus took pity on the driver, bidding him stop, volunteering to make what remained of the trip on foot. At the rate they were inching forward, he was confident he could outpace the horses anyway. It was just as well he thought so, because hardly a moment after he climbed down from the cab, they spooked and bolted, proving just how much they'd been holding back all along. He could still hear the rumor of their shrill whinnying as he tromped up the path, his tiny shoes making a wet crunching noise on the spotless, shimmering, alien turf that was quickly accumulating. When he finally threw open the rusty gates, he dislodged piles of the stuff that clung to the tops of the iron bars like a loose white moss. He frowned at the sight of it, not so much disgusted as deeply mystified. It had a strange way of making him feel warmer, even as it confirmed how impossibly cold it was outside...

Snow, he thought, marveling. *Snow in St. Argonsburg*...

For a moment, he looked up at the Worlds... wondering. But finally, he shook his head. He could consider whether to redraw the lines between fact and fiction later...

He ran the rest of the way through the starfield of fresh little flakes up to the towering Manor, spouting a misty trail of hot breath. He paused to pant a brief spell, even as two soldiers approached him from their posts at the door...

"Stay right there," one of them instructed. "State your business."

"I'm Horus Templar," he explained between gasps of air. "I'm here to see my client."

They looked at each other with worried expressions. "You may have a hard time doing that, Sir. The Baron... he's just come up missing. The rest of my men are searching the grounds, even as we speak."

"You've *got* to be kidding," Horus said, ready to collapse.

"I wish I was, Sir. All we could find of him was this note..."

"Let me see that," Horus said, accepting the tiny piece of paper. His eyes zoomed across the wiggly scrawling...

Gone fishing, back in five minutes. Sincerely yours, His High Excellentness, Dukiest of Dukes, Baron Von Tweed

"For the life of me, I don't know how he could've escaped," the soldier went on. "We had men posted at every access point... under every window..."

Horus looked back up, his heavy breathing arrested for a moment. "But he *hasn't* escaped," he said. "Don't you see? He's still in the castle!"

The soldier eyed him questioningly. "There's no fish to be had in the castle. Are you sure, Sir?"

Horus nodded emphatically. "It's a feint. I know how he thinks. Sort of... hopefully. If he says he's gone, that's precisely where he isn't."

The military men exchanged another look. "Should we alert the other men?" the subordinate of the two asked his superior.

"By all means, go get them!" Horus insisted. "I'll find the Baron myself."

"I hope you can, Sir. It'll be all our heads if he gets away."

"He won't. But hurry; get the other guards!"

The soldier nodded. "Good luck in there. If the Baron's half as crafty as you suppose, you'll need it."

* * *

For as spooky as it was in the daytime, the inner courtyard was twice as bad at night. One small step out from under the overhanging balcony of the upper story, past the crisp line on the ground of collecting snow, and Horus had the distinct feeling that he'd just crossed the threshold into the heart of darkness. He couldn't smell Tweed... truthfully, he couldn't smell anything beyond some strange, pervasive odor of burnt sea-cucumber. Nevertheless, his instincts all agreed... he was *here*...

"You can't hide, Tweed," he called out, taking one slow, cautious step after another into the ranks of ruined sculpture all around him. A frigid breeze prickled him between the raised hairs on the back of his neck. But he remained calm, deliberate as his eyes scanned the scene. "I know you're out there..."

"That's okay," the voice of Tweed answered, from nowhere in particular, and with a new edge of creepiness. "I know *you're* out there, too..."

Horus pressed forward, searching down a row between statues. "I've come to end this," he said. "Stop playing games."

"But the game has just begun." Horus failed to whirl fast enough, catching only the faintest glimpse of movement out of the corner of his eye. "You may have found me, but you'll never catch me. I'm a phantasm... a rouge shadow in the night. I'm a whisper on the wind. How can you hope to lay hold of what isn't there?"

There was another flash of action in the distance. Only this time, Horus was looking in exactly the right direction to see Tweed skulk between pillars, all in a silly, hunched tiptoe. Horus blinked as all apprehension flew away like an unstopped balloon.

"Tweed, I can clearly see you out there."

"...No you can't." He slunk by again in full view.

Horus sighed. "Well, it doesn't matter. We can have this conversation face to face, or we can have it shouting back and forth across the courtyard. Either way, we've come to the end of your hijinks. I solved the riddle, Tweed. I know what you did."

Tweed laughed menacingly. "Back with another silly theory, eh, Mr. Templar? Go ahead; let's hear it. Amuse your Baron."

Horus rolled his jaw; he deplored to be so taunted. If he was wrong this time, he was sure he'd never live it down. But now was no time to doubt himself. This was what he'd come for. He drew himself up very straight...

"There was never any killing," he announced confidently. "Never. We haven't failed to come up with a victim because of any special incompetence on our part... nor any great cleverness on yours. We haven't found a victim because there isn't one. There never was."

For a while, the silence and stillness of the snowfield prevailed. Tweed was speechless. Horus couldn't help being a bit amazed himself. He was sure: He'd struck a nerve...

"That's a pretty serious accusation," Tweed said at last. "I hope for your sake you can prove it."

Horus shook his head at the emptiness before him. "I don't have to. It's only a question of showing reasonable doubt. That much, I can do."

"I'd like to see you try," Tweed challenged.

"Then let me break it down for you," Horus said, starting again in the direction of Tweed's voice. "First, there was the matter of *the look*."

"The look?" Tweed repeated with contempt.

"Yes. I gave you a *look* in court that was meant to compel you to tell the truth. But later, after you'd confessed, Blackforest gave you the same *look*... yet for all his skill and determination, he couldn't coax the rest of the truth out of you. He couldn't get you to name your victim. It begs the question: What's the contradiction? Why should one *look* succeed, and the other fail? Unless, of course, you had never actually succumbed to the look to start with..."

"A *conclusion*, Mr. Templar," Tweed bandied. "A hasty one at that. You're off to a bad start."

"There's more," Horus promised, zeroing-in on a rusty old knight suit a few rows ahead of him. "I had your handwriting examined by an SAPD graphologist. His findings support my conclusion. Try though he might, he couldn't attach a name to the big secret you've been keeping."

"Graphology?!" Tweed demanded, his elbow protruding into view from behind the suit of armor as he put his hands on his hips. "Are you joking? Even I know that stuff is inadmissible in court. It's incompetent." As Horus drew near, they now faced each other, with Tweed making no further effort to slip away again. "Really, Mr. Templar, it sounds like you have nothing to make your case at all."

"Very well," Horus allowed. "Let's take a moment to examine *your* side of things. You say you killed a man. What do *you* offer as proof? There's not a shred of physical evidence to support your claim. Even laying aside the matter of corpus delicti, we had the best medical mind in the department check you over, head-to-toe. She found no foreign blood, no gunpowder or other chemical residue. So you see, the prosecution is no better off than I am."

Tweed maintained a blank look for a moment. Then, his face curled up in an awful grin. "You almost had me worried for a second there. But you're forgetting one major piece of evidence, Mr. Templar... something you've evidently forgotten about ever since you got that wild idea that I killed my grandfather. You're forgetting the *bruises*! The ones all up and down my arms!"

Horus promptly smiled back. "But I didn't forget them, Tweed."

Tweed frowned. "No? Then why didn't you mention them?"

"Because," Horus explained, leaning forward in a belittling sort of way. "I was hoping *you* would." He turned on his heel, pacing back away with his hands folded behind his back. "Hoping you would commit to the narrative of a recent killing by invoking the single most conspicuous red herring of this entire case," he went on, before pivoting back. "The *bruises*. How do you propose to have incurred them, Tweed? Were they defensive? Did your victim try to beat your hands off of him when you strangled him?"

"Y...yes," Tweed agreed weakly, nodding afterwards. "That was it, of course!"

Horus shook his head. "Impossible. Your arms would've been bruised on the *top* side."

Tweed blanched. "I... he... I b...bludgeoned him with my arms! Yeah! That's what I did!"

"Hm," Horus mused. "A strange way to kill someone, but certainly possible. Yet even that fails to explain how you passed the foreign blood test."

"I..." Tweed faltered. "I..."

"How is my case looking now, Tweed?"

The little man's eyes darted all about; he was in a panic. "You... you'll never win!" he asserted. "I still have my confession! It's my word against yours!"

"Ah, yes... the word of a crazy man," Horus framed it. "The word that set this whole misadventure in motion. The funny thing is, of course, we've known you were mad from the start. You made no bones about it. We *thought* we'd accounted for it. We thought we knew better than to trust a word you said. And yet, all along, there was one thing you told us that we never stopped to question... one thing we consistently took for granted: The validity of your confession. After all, *no one* would confess to a crime that never happened. No one, that is, except for you. No one except Arcadian Tweed."

Tweed stared. He didn't breathe. He didn't blink. But finally – slowly – his features brightened. A look of admiration came over him, like a magician who'd just had his greatest card trick explained to him by a stranger. There was something unmistakably genuine about the twinkle in his eye... and perhaps a bit menacing. "Well, well," he chuckled. "What can I say? You got me, Mr. Templar. You caught me in the act. But now, be honest... can you *really* blame me for trying? Think of it: I got to be a murderer without even having to kill anybody! It was the perfect crime!"

Horus sighed… at once relieved to have coaxed out the mystery, and yet again bewildered at this endlessly vexing man. "Yes… you're certainly your own breed of criminal-mastermind. Now, come along, Tweed… we need to get this all sorted out back at Headquarters. It's been a long, harrowing evening, and I'm ready to be out of the cold…"

Even as Horus began to tromp away, he noted that Tweed didn't follow…

"If you don't mind, Mr. Templar, I'd like to ask *you* a question first."

Horus stopped, not quite looking back over his shoulder. "Yes?"

"I couldn't help noticing that you came here *alone*…" Tweed said. "That was kind of impulsive, wasn't it? Did you even tell anyone else what you figured out? Or, did you just come running as fast as you could get here?"

"I…" Horus began, forced to admit to himself that he may've erred. "As a matter of fact, I might've been a bit hasty…"

"Now don't be taciturn, Horus," Tweed said, leaning against the armor suit he'd earlier been hiding behind. "I admitted *my* secret. So tell me straight: Does a single person in the world besides you know that I'm innocent?"

Horus turned back, eyeing Tweed. "No. Not yet. What of it?"

Tweed shrugged. "I was just thinking. Thinking it might be nice if no one ever *did* find out…"

Horus frowned. He started for Tweed, intent to drag him out of the courtyard, if necessary. "Now look, Tweed, it's time you…"

He stopped short as Tweed leapt back, drawing a knife out of the armor suit in the same action. "Ah… looky here," he said, the light of the Other Worlds glinting on the blade. "Would you believe the things these empty old knight suits leave lying around sometimes? Someone really *could* get hurt…"

Horus extended a hand in warning. "Put that away, Tweed. You've already caused your share of mischief. Don't dream up anything now that you can't walk away from."

"Who said anything about walking away?" Tweed asked, fiddling with the long knife as he slowly encroached on Horus. "A man's got to have his priorities. He's got to protect his secrets. I didn't murder anyone, Mr. Templar. That's my secret. And it happens to be a very, *very* good secret. Maybe the best secret of all time." He raised the knife as his eyes burned with a crazed intent, and Horus knew he'd crossed the brink. "A secret worth killing for…"

Tweed threw himself into a leaping lunge. Horus only made it halfway into a defensive posture when suddenly, with his would-be killer still careening through the air, he was stricken dumb by a deafening peal of thunder...

KWTAAAAAAAAAAAAAAAAaaaaaaaaap

He blinked his way through a blinding flash only just soon enough to watch some final arcs course over Tweed's body. The little man fell back in nearly the direction he'd sprung, landing in a convulsing heap in the snow. Horus watched him stop twitching... saw his muscles relax as his eyes shut. He was out cold...

For his part, Horus was hardly less stunned. After moments of careful scrutiny, he did the only thing he could think to do... he looked up into the sky – where lightning is wont to come from. The Other Worlds were there, of course... all lined up... and not a storm cloud in sight. Had he... had he just been saved by some sort of paranormal manifestation? *Preposterous*. Surely, utterly preposterous...

Fortunately, this proved to be very much the case. As Horus finished turning around, he looked back down, just below eye-level. And there – almost directly behind him – he found Deputy Constable Miloje, standing in a long coat, cool as can be. He was holding out a finger-gun...

"Good evening, Counselor," Miloje greeted him, holstering his hand.

Horus nodded. "Milo." He took a moment to look back at Tweed, still splayed out on the ground, steam rising from his prone form wherever the snow landed on him. He turned another questioning glance at Miloje. "Was that...?"

"Yes," Miloje answered. "I was sent with the District Attorney's blessing to serve the Baron his eviction notice. Seems I arrived just in time to hear you coax his deep dark secret out of him. Very fortuitous timing on my part, it would appear. At least, for you. I might've preferred that *my own* secret remain intact. But of course, even in solving our mystery for us, you would have to find a way to spoil *something*..."

Horus shook his head, still in disbelief. "Well, I appreciate what you did... however you did it. But you know, it really wasn't necessary. I had the situation well in hand."

Miloje huffed. "Allowing a maniac with a knife to leap on you is hardly what I would call having the situation in hand. You're welcome anyway."

Horus turned his eyes down to Tweed yet again. "Will he be alright?"

"Not to worry," Miloje assured him. "He'll be back to his intolerable self in plenty of time for you to clear him of all wrong-doing." He grinned mischievously at Horus. "That is, unless you intend to press charges for attempted murder."

Horus shook his head. "I don't think so, Milo. Perhaps as a pretense to get him into court, if I really must. But he'll be no danger anymore, once his secret is public knowledge."

Miloje shrugged. "Leave it to you to take a nauseatingly humanitarian stance like that. Why should I expect anything more?"

"Well, I *am* his attorney," Horus reminded him with a grin. "Come on. Let's get him back to the station."

"Agreed. My old bones can't take this cold..."

Chapter 17

KNOCK KNOCK KNOCK

Judge Felix jolted awake at the sound of rapping on his chamber door. With an inaudible groan and a quick scratch behind the ear, he made his way in the dark to answer it...

"Sorry to wake you, your Honor," one of the judicial secretaries announced as soon as the door cracked open. "Something's come up rather suddenly."

"Charis, it's practically the middle of the night," Felix explained, all drooping eyelids. "Who would demand an audience at this hour?"

"It's Horus Templar, Sir."

Felix sighed. "Of course it is." He scratched around the collar of his nightgown, turning back into his room. "I'll be out in ten minutes." He went to go throw on a robe and a wig...

* * *

Horus no sooner set his briefcase on the table than he noticed the judge shambling out of his chambers. He looked up, grinning nervously when he saw who it was. *Naturally they'd bother Felix with this*, he thought...

"Good evening, your Honor," he said.

"It's *night* for me, thank you," Felix replied. "What is this all about, Horus?"

"It's the Tweed investigation," Horus explained. "It's come suddenly to a head."

Felix's ears stood fully upright. "Tweed, you say? Really? You've learned who he killed, then?"

"Well..." Horus hesitated. "The answer is both yes and no. We'll be sure it all comes out in direct examination. But in fact, Tweed's been arraigned on an entirely separate charge. He's accused of the *attempted* murder of a public servant."

Felix blinked. "Strange. But, alright. Who did he *try* to kill?"

"Me."

"Imagine that," Felix said, taking one more step for the bench before he froze in his tracks, throwing up his hands. "Wait. *Wait*. We're not really going to do *this* again, are we?" He turned a demanding look back at Horus.

"What do you mean?"

"I mean *you*," Felix explained. "An encore of your one-man show. Horus the defense attorney... Horus the *plaintiff*. I suppose you mean to be the prosecution again, as well..."

"You needn't worry about that," Blucille Cordon announced, hurrying on her heels down the aisle. "I can assure you the State is every bit as anxious to settle this as Mr. Templar himself."

Horus gave her a smile and a nod before turning back to Felix. "Actually, your Honor, I did consider the possibility that you might be called on, and I've taken additional measures to spare you undue frustration. My part in this case will really be quite small, as the defense has nothing to present. Any relevant information not introduced by the prosecution will be handled by amicus curiae."

"Amicus curiae? Who are you talking about?"

A second briefcase joined Horus' on the table. His eyes snapped down to it, tracing up the white sleeve to behold the amicus curiae himself...

"Eb Thalymus, yer Honor... ready and rarin' ta provide supplemental counsel."

"*Thalymus*," Felix repeated weakly, resting his head on his hand. "A *great* improvement. But very well. Bring forth the accused."

* * *

"It was just like that, Ms. Cordon," Deputy Constable Miloje testified. "When I came up on them, Mr. Templar was already in the midst of a heated exchange with his client."

"And, in the course of this discussion, what more did you witness?" Blucille asked.

"Just a moment, yer Honor," Eb interjected, rising from his seat. "The friend o' the court is aware o' this conversation what took place betwixt the plaintiff and the defendant. It is our intention ta examine the content of said conversation in greater d'tail, so thet the defendant may be cleared of other pending charges against hisself."

Felix turned to Cordon. "Does the prosecution have any objections to opening this line of questioning?"

"None whatsoever, your Honor," she grinned.

"*Alright*," Felix shrugged. "The amicus curiae may proceed."

Eb approached the witness stand. "Naw, Mr. Miloje, would ya please relate to the court exactly what it was ya overheard when y'all approached the scene?"

"Gladly, I would," Miloje nodded. "Mr. Templar spoke of the 'one thing we took for granted: The validity of your confession.' The defendant's confession to an alleged killing, that is. It is a matter of public record."

"I und'rstand," Eb went along. "What more did Mr. Templar have ta say?"

"He went on to retort that, '*No one* would confess to a crime that never happened. No one, except Arcadian Tweed,' he said."

"An' how did the defendant react ta this statement?"

"He confirmed Templar's allegation. He admitted that his confessed killing was a sham. A hoax. 'I didn't murder anyone, Mr. Templar.' Those were his exact words. 'That's my secret,' he said. 'A secret worth killing for.' That was when he leapt at the plaintiff, wielding a knife."

"There, naw," Eb smiled, gently slapping the stand. He looked up at Felix. "Yer Honor, I do apologize if the matter o' this separate, fallacious killin' seems irrelevant and immaterial. However, it is ma contention thet we should clear the air surroundin' this first allegation here an' now, since it is a prominent matter – a peculiar matter – one that Mr. Tweed cannot be formally arraigned on, since – as we jist established – the en-tire crime exists – and has only ever existed – in the imagination of Tweed, hisself. It is a fiction – one thet Mr. Tweed clung to with such desperation, thet he ultimately attempted murder, jist so's he could stop his fib from gittin' debunked. It is thus that I implore the court to formally dismiss all suspicion related to Mr. Tweed, regardin' this first confessed killin'. For it is only by the court's rulin' that the police investigation may be officially closed. Furthermore, it is with a mind fer the welfare o' the Jast-Madiiran constit'ency thet I..."

"Just a moment, Mr. Thalymus," Felix interjected. "You're asking me to throw out Tweed's original killing scandal – the one the Deputy Constable just testified was a lie. Is that all?"

Eb nodded. "Yes, yer Honor."

"Well, no need to make a speech about it," Felix said, raising and clacking his gavel. "I hereby commute Arcadian Tweed for the murder he didn't commit, which he first claimed he did. Now, can we please commence with the case at hand?"

Horus, along with most of the players in the case, took a moment to catch Tweed's reaction. They watched him wilt silently in his chair...

Eb turned to Blucille. "I believe the floor is yours agin, Ms. Cordon."

"Thank you, Mr. Thalymus," she said, returning to the stand as he retired. "Now, Mr. Miloje, where did we leave off? You witnessed a discussion between the plaintiff and the defendant."

"Yes," Miloje answered. "As I said, it turned dangerously violent soon after I arrived. The defendant had a knife. He leapt at the defendant while brandishing it. I'm afraid Mr. Templar was quite at his mercy. It was at that moment that I..." he cleared his throat, "*...stepped in*."

"I see," Blucille replied. She looked up at the judge. "I believe we've shown intent here. My thanks to the amicus curiae for thoroughly addressing any question of motive. I suppose all that remains is the physical evidence." She produced a big knife, showing it to Miloje. "Is this the knife the defendant was wielding?"

"It is," Miloje confirmed.

She nodded, stepping away. "I will have this stamped as State's Exhibit A, after which, the prosecution rests its case."

"Does the defense wish to cross-examine this witness?" Felix asked.

Horus rose. "No, your Honor. Furthermore, the defense has no case to present, as previously stated."

"Hm," Felix mused, stroking his whiskers. "This trial is certainly not without room for prejudicial misconduct. It tends to invite bias, when the defense lawyer is also the intended victim. I do wonder if other counsel should've been appointed..."

After a beat where everyone held their breath, Felix continued. "...However, the body of evidence against the defendant is indeed damaging. I fail to see how any retrial could materially affect the obvious ruling." He clacked his gavel. "The defendant Arcadian Tweed is found guilty of one count of Attempted Murder."

"Just a moment, your Honor!" Horus interjected.

Felix shot him a look. "What *now*, Mr. Templar? Your window to present a defense is closed. You closed it yourself."

"I speak now as the plaintiff, your Honor," Horus explained. "Being, with regard to the law, the injured party here, and seeing that the accused has been formally tried and found guilty, I no longer wish to pursue charges. I harbor no ill-will for Mr. Tweed, and I would have him commuted. I ask that the court consider this before pronouncing sentence."

Felix shook his head. “You’re really playing your prejudicial privileges from both sides, aren’t you? You got him convicted, now you’re trying to stop him being sentenced. What do you *want*, Templar?”

“Something less serious than execution, if I may be so bold,” he answered. “Tweed ultimately failed to kill me; I would hardly find it equitable to demand his life of him now.”

Felix turned to Blucille. “What does the prosecution prescribe?”

Blucille shrugged. “Community service?”

“Very well.” Felix struck the bench again. “The man Arcadian Tweed is sentenced to a life term of community service.” He squinted at Horus. “I trust that is more to the plaintiff’s liking?” It was more a command than a question.

“Certainly, your Honor,” Horus went along whole-heartedly.

“Then it is done. Let the accused begin his sentence at once.”

Unbidden, Tweed rose in address, the chains around his arms jingling. “I have only one thing to say first,” he announced. “One thing you all must know. I am *not* the man you know as Arcadian Tweed,” he explained solemnly. “I am… a visitor from another world…”

“Get him out of here!” Miloje hastened the bailiffs. The next moment, they had him by the arms, hauling him out…

“You can’t do this to me!” Tweed demanded, kicking and jostling. “You can’t just let me off with a slap on the wrist! I *had* you! I had you all convinced that I committed the crime of the century! And I would’ve gotten away with it, too, if it weren’t for you meddling dogs and your kid!!”

Horus sighed in relief as he watched the crazy little man be enveloped by a tidal wave of reporters, just beyond the doors…

“Court is dismissed,” Felix said as he stood, before he slowly began to plod away. *“And I’m going back to bed…”* he muttered…

* * *

Horus was slow in making his departure. There seemed quite a lot to reflect on. It was another one of those cases he’d both won and lost. He’d played pretty fast and loose in the end; he couldn’t help feeling a bit sloppy. But, as he carefully closed his briefcase – the one he’d had no actual need to open in the first place – he decided that he really did feel good about the way everything turned out. He’d spared a client, and – with any good fortune – ended a city-wide delirium. But most of all, he’d uncovered the *truth*... in one of the strangest hiding places it had ever wandered off to, no less. No self-respecting attorney could help a warm and fuzzy feeling about something like that...

"Congratulations on another implausible success, Templar," Miloje said, approaching the defense table. Horus was a bit surprised; in his moment of introspection, he'd supposed everyone else had left the court. Why did Miloje remain behind? But even as he wondered, he arrived at a likely answer...

"Some of the congratulations belong to you, Milo," Horus replied.

"Is that a thank-you for saving your pelt?"

Horus shook his head. "I maintain that I could've fended Tweed off myself. I'm not as helpless as I appear. But that's really beside the point. You *are* the hero in this, Milo. Your testimony was the only thing that made it all possible."

"I know it well," Miloje said, examining his curled fingers nonchalantly. "And I credit you for being humble enough to admit it." He looked directly at Horus. "Even so, you *stymie* me, Templar. An inquisitive fellow like you should certainly have asked about the elephant in the room by now."

"I'm not sure what you mean," Horus grinned.

"*Indeed*," Miloje huffed. "I shoot a man out of the air with a bolt of lightning, and it fails to rate as even a trifling curiosity to you?"

Horus chuckled. "Alright, I confess... it really is a head-scratcher. But I think I can safely deduce that it was accomplished with magic."

Miloje nodded. "That's right. But you were there, at the trade show. You'll remember it took two peddlers to accomplish the same trick I performed myself."

"Yes, I do recall. They explained that electricity requires both Positive and Negative Magic. They also said that if a person tries to imbibe two types of magic, one will simply overwrite the other." Horus thought about it quietly for a moment, scratching under his chin, before he simply threw his hands up. "You got me, Milo. You've obviously outfoxed the best experts on the subject I've ever come across. I can't reckon how you did it."

"You'll kick yourself when you learn how simple it was," Miloje said, resting his hands on the table. Then, he raised one hand, about a foot above the board. "Let's say I drink this much Positive elixir... as much as I dare to chance." He raised his other hand, lower than the first. "Then, all I have to do is down half as much Negative. Two magics, in equilibrium, all in one sorcerer. It is only a matter of getting the right dosage, in the right order."

Horus shook his head. "That *is* remarkable." He leaned forward. "I suppose this also accounts for your miraculous recovery from heart arrythmia?"

"Of course," Miloje confirmed. "That was the whole impetus to getting magic in the first place. I can regulate my own heartbeat now without so much as a thought." He smiled deviously. "If, through no fault of my own, I get to enjoy a few other powers besides, it can hardly be helped."

"I'm sure you don't mind knowing you can out-draw anyone in St. Argonsburg," Horus quipped.

Miloje made a finger-gun, winking. "Fastest finger on the force," he said.

Horus grabbed up his briefcase, making ready to go. "I'm only sorry I hampered you, learning about the trick up your sleeve."

"Not at all," Miloje replied, as they both began to walk out. "I've quite enjoyed this opportunity to extol my own genius. If anything, it was surely overdue." But he looked very serious at Horus. "Just see that you don't spread it around. We old policemen need our aces in the hole."

"Don't worry," Horus said. "Your secret's safe with me."

* * *

Shortly after dawn, reinforcements met Horus at Civil HQ, bearing good tidings. Deborah slapped the morning paper on Horus' chest as they met in the lobby. "Looks like our case made front-page news again, Boss. I hope you're ready for a shock."

Horus took the paper, unrolling it. "The Syzygy Killer – A Fraud." He folded it down, nodding. "Now, that is rather surprising."

"Why's thet?" Eb asked, as he and Art drew into the huddle. "I'd say we done plenty ta prove it."

"We did," Horus agreed. "I'm only surprised that the newsmen would admit it."

Eb smiled, shaking his head. "Golly, Horus, but I'm beholden to ya. It shore was nice gettin' a piece o' the action agin! But ya know, there's a reason I ain' had many cases in a span. I jist ain't got the starch I used ta have. So, I been thinkin': When we's partners, I hope ya don't mind if I serves mostly in an advisory capacity; lendin' helpful hints, now an' agin. How's that grab ya?"

Horus looked uncomfortably at Deborah, who returned the expression. "Well, Eb... about that partnership," Horus began, hating himself. "Working this case with you has been an honor and a privilege… truly! But I've been thinking about your proposition, as well… and I'm afraid I must insist that if we *are* to incorporate, then we're going to have to lay down some ground rules…"

Just as Eb began to look truly blindsided, Art suddenly leapt in front of Horus. "Pardon me, Mr. Thalymus, but I think what Horus meant to say is that he doesn't want you entering into anything willy-nilly. Not when he knows there are other opportunities you might like even better."

Everyone regarded Art with deep perplexity. "Other opportunities?" Eb asked at length. "What're we talkin', here?"

"Well, I couldn't help noticing the way you're always harping on youngins," Art explained, borrowing a bit of the parlance. "The thing is, if you work with Horus, you're really cheating yourself."

"I am?" Eb asked.

"Yes, I think you are. After all, Horus is a busy man… a full-time professional. And there's only so many hours of the day you can spend badgering just one man."

"Yes," Horus nodded emphatically. "That really *is* what I was driving at."

"So here's the counterproposal…" Art went on. "Did you ever think about becoming an adjunct law professor?"

Eb looked on with wide eyes. "Why… why, no," he admitted. "It never even crossed ma mind."

Art wrapped one arm around Eb's shoulder, gesturing out with the other. "Picture this, Mr. Thalymus: You could share your life story with hundreds of people on a daily basis. Rooms and rooms full of empty-headed kids who'd be forced to listen to you. What could be a more perfect vision than that?"

"Jeepers criminy," Eb intoned, almost trance-like. "It's beauteeful." He blinked, and glanced questioningly at Art. "But I'm a lawman, not an ejimacator. I can' jist waltz in there an' demand a faculty position."

"You could if you wanted," Art shrugged. "I already talked with the local Anubican campus. They'd be happy to have someone on with your experience."

"Wahl, if thet don't beat all!" Eb said, snapping his fingers. But then, he quickly looked sobered again, turning to Horus. "But naw, the decision has ta be yours, Horus. If you was countin' on ma help, I shore don't mean ta leave ya in a lurch."

Horus gave him an affirming pat on the shoulder. “Go ahead, Eb. Live the dream.”

Eb clapped his hands together. “Say no more! It’s been a pleasure, y’all!” he said, shaking each of their hands in turn. “We’ll do supper some time. We’ll keep in touch. But fer now, I gots ta get goin’. There’s youngin’s thet need learnin’, and I’s jist the one ta give it to ‘em!”

As Eb whisked himself away, Deborah turned to Art, mouthing a silent ‘thank you’. Art only nodded.

“Well, it’s only a shame Eb couldn’t stay for breakfast,” Horus segued. “We’ve finally come to the end of this three-ring circus. How better to celebrate than gorging ourselves?”

“Works for me,” Art agreed. “I’ll even front the dough...”

But before they could begin to hash out the specifics, they were stopped short by a distant call...

“Mr. Templar!” they heard. “Mr. Templar, Sir!” It was Captain Alexei, barreling up to them...

“What is it, Alexei?” Horus asked, just as the captain arrived in their midst.

“There is a matter that begs your attention, Sir,” he replied, quickly catching his breath. “But I see you have the paper; perhaps you are already aware.”

Horus grimaced. “I don’t understand,” he admitted. “Tweed was outed for his lie. Shouldn’t that be the end of it?”

Alexei shook his head. “I don’t mean anything about Tweed. Did you happen to see what was on page seven?”

Horus laughed nervously. “No, indeed. I’m sure I wouldn’t have even thought to look.” He flipped through the paper and scanned the page, quickly finding what Alexei meant for him to see. “High Constable to Deliver Speech...” he read aloud.

“He’s going through with it,” Deborah marveled.

“When is this?” Horus asked.

“In just over an hour, at the Grufthoffen Stalag,” Alexei explained, referring to his watch. “I was tasked with ensuring your attendance.”

“I wouldn’t miss it,” Horus replied. “Let’s go.”

* * *

"I don't believe it's at all presumptuous to suggest that the highest honor belongs to the one who makes the noblest sacrifice," High Constable Amadeus recited. His voice echoed throughout the assembly with gravitas befitting the words... an *authenticity* – almost – which was only undermined by the way he read the speech directly from the page. Horus fancied it might not have been so bad, if Amadeus could've at least left the speech on the podium. He held it no more than a few inches from his face...

"This life we live, demands much of all of us," he continued. "We each have responsibilities we are entrusted with. We each have our load to carry. But few are those who can rival the uniquely solemn charge of the *soldier*. It is the soldier we ask to stand in the gulf for us. It is the soldier we entrust to strive in our stead, to protect the foundations we all depend on. At times, we bid him face evils and terrors the likes of which we can hardly imagine. And dutifully, he does. He faces doubt, grief, and turmoil. He faces *death*. He gives his life, so that others may live. Truly, he makes the noblest sacrifice of all."

Amadeus flung up one hand, gesturing lazily behind him, even as he kept his eyes trained on the paper. "It is with this sacrifice in mind that we gather here today... to honor our fighting men by redeeming them from their long captivity. We show our gratitude to the living, vowing never to forget the dead. We bestow on them both honor and goodwill, such as we can... and we leave the rest in the hands of the Creators."

Finally, he turned to face the front gate of the Stalag. "Lieutenant Colonel Elitis, lead your men out of camp!" he called.

The gate opened, and out marched Elitis in full dress uniform, with his men following in two long ranks. Everyone clapped and cheered. And somehow, through all the fanfare and motion, Elitis caught a glimpse of Horus in the crowd. He nodded. Horus nodded back...

"You did very well by these men, Mr. Templar," Alexei said, as they watched the parade. "We don't get many speeches in Podunkville, but I am sure this was a fine one indeed. And it is wonderful to see so many restored to their full honor and standing."

Deborah looked Alexei's uniform up and down. "Speaking of full honor and standing, I'm glad to see Stenya didn't actually dress you down, Alexei. I noticed you still have all your stripes."

"Indeed," Alexei replied. "I count myself incredibly fortunate that I wasn't demoted."

Horus blinked, looking over at the two of them. "Demoted? I didn't know you were in any kind of trouble..."

"*Heh*, yes," Alexei grinned nervously. "I, eh, won't get into the particulars, but it was touch-and-go for a bit. The Deputy Constable certainly had me believing I had lost my position as his successor. He had me imagining every sort of trouble for myself, truth be told... for so he invited me, when he neglected to mention what manner of punishment he intended."

"What *did* he end up doing to you, if you don't mind my asking?" Deborah ventured.

"Not a thing," Alexei answered. "Besides let me stew in my own dread of what he *would* do. That was my penance, he said."

"I think that's wise," Horus commented. "Anyway, it seems to reinforce the same general maxim as everything else to come out of this Syzygy scare. Sometimes the imagination really is the worst tormentor."

"As you say, Mr. Templar, Sir," Alexei went along. "Really, it just left me feeling that the Deputy Constable is quite poor at contriving appropriate disciplinary action."

"Horus..." Deborah said suddenly, quietly. She turned from the pageant to look at him. He was taken aback by her sudden intensity...

"Yes, Deborah?"

"Well, while we're on the subject... I have... something I should tell you. Something I should've trusted you with a while back."

Now, Horus was really shaken. He had no idea what uncomfortable thing she was about to share... and that was indeed a torment...

"What is it?"

"*Ugh*, I'm out of my mind to tell you this..." she groaned. "You know how Art's been checking into something for me? I mean, surely you guessed as much, with all we've been in contact. Not to mention the fact that he's basically the most indiscreet person on the planet."

"I did note... *something*, of course," he admitted. "What about it?"

"Well, you see..." she started. "I didn't want you to know, because I know how rational you are. You would've thought I was crazy." She laughed mirthlessly as she stroked her ears back. "Now you're going to anyway..."

"Deborah..." he said gently. "What's the matter?"

"I thought I was turning into a Werehuman!" she blurted. "The clammy skin, the blunted face, the whole nine yards. I grew up believing it was in my family history, and I've been sick over it all week!"

"You..." Horus started, mystified. "You wanted Art to find out if you were... *transforming*?"

"I thought if I just knew for sure one way or the other, I could get past this," she explained. "That is, once I was sure I hadn't eaten someone."

"*Eaten*?"

"But after all this time, I still don't have a shred of proof. I don't have anything to tell me definitely that Werehumans are real. And I've just been beside myself, worrying you'd find out I actually thought I was mutating into a monster at night!" She shook her head. "So, tell me honestly, Horus: Isn't that the silliest thing you ever heard of?"

He took it all in for a moment, while she watched anxiously for his reaction. Then, he slowly smiled, and nodded. "Oh, it's silly alright," he said.

She sighed, turning away. "I knew it."

"...Silly that you could honestly believe something like this would make me think any less of you," he went on.

She looked back at him.

"We all have our quirks, Deborah... and we all have trouble deciphering reality from fantasy at times. I don't doubt your judgement, and I don't doubt *you*. Remember that."

She smiled, looking down. "Thank you, Horus. It means a lot. I really should've listened to Art and told you upfront. A lot of people suffered for my superstition. I did. Art did. Blucille and Captain Alexei. Really the whole city when I think about it." She shook her head. "And that poor woman, Hailey Barborough. Tackled in the middle of the night... just because I don't know an urban legend when I hear one..."

"Funny thing about her..." Alexei mused.

They both looked over at him. "What do you mean?" Deborah asked.

"Well, you know, the incident really stuck with me... it was I who tackled her, after all. I thought to look her up... to see if I might apologize more thoroughly for the whole misunderstanding. So, I ran her name at the Dronehood office. And do you know what I learned?"

"What?" Deborah asked with bated breath.

"There is no woman by the name of 'Hailey Barborough' in St. Argonsburg. Nor in all of Jast-Madiir. There never has been."

Horus and Deborah exchanged a very doubtful look...

Acknowledgments

My thanks, as always, go out to John and Rachael V. and their family for being dependable troves of information and inspiration... and to my mom, for the indispensable service of her proofreading, and all the hours she spent listening to me talk about the exceedingly random garbage that was so central to this tale. I owe my dad an enormous amount of gratitude for offering up the idea of the courtroom heckler... the absolute perfect starting point for this book. Special thanks also go out to Rebekka Rochelle Moreno, who persistently assured me that this story was coming along just fine, even when I knew my progress was absolutely glacial.

I should certainly thank Andy Griffith. I never did commit to watching his serialized court drama; it just struck me as a little too modern and edgy. Nevertheless, the television commercials alone proved that the southern-gentleman-lawyer was too tantalizing of an archetype to leave unexplored.

I have thanked Michael Crichton in the past, but obviously, this is another story that benefited enormously from one or more of his dino-novels. I owe a shout-out to the minds behind Hogans Heroes and Scooby Doo, too.

My thanks to popular science in general for providing all the inspiration I would ever have needed to write Silbadilio's scene, and then some. Ditto for modern journalism.

For More from E.L. Ward…

Visit his personal site, at:

https://www.booksofelward.com

His vast arsenal of backlist titles includes the following:

TITLES IN THE ORPHAN UNIVERSE

HERON PROPHECIES SERIES

The Chocolate Prophecy

HORUS TEMPLAR – PUBLIC DEFENDER SERIES

Horus Templar and the Case of the Wimpy War-Criminal
Horus Templar and the Case of the Iniquitous Inquisitor
Horus Templar and the Case of the Draft-Dodging Drone
Horus Templar and the Case of the Dubious Decedent
Horus Templar and the Case of the Vengeful Vigilant

E.L. Ward is proud to partner with:

MALOB ARTS

Check out his and other creative works at:

www.malobarts.com

Made in the USA
Monee, IL
04 November 2026

67386062R10105